John Allegro [illegible] University in 1951 with a first-class honours degree in philology. Two years later, he became the first British member of the international team of experts assigned to decipher and edit the Dead Sea Scrolls, and his later book on the subject was an international bestseller.

In 1970, his *The Sacred Mushroom and the Cross* made a sensational popular impact, but drew a torrent of flak from the scholarly establishment. This book, the fruit of fourteen years of etymological research, is likely to prove equally controversial.

'A man with an original mind who is prepared to stimulate and shock.' *Guardian*

Also by John Allegro in ABACUS:

THE SACRED MUSHROOM AND THE CROSS

John Allegro

LOST GODS

ABACUS

ABACUS edition published in 1978
by Sphere Books Ltd
30/32 Gray's Inn Road, London WC1X 8JL

First published in Great Britain
by Michael Joseph Ltd 1977

Set in Intertype Times

*Printed in Great Britain by Cox & Wyman Ltd,
London, Reading and Fakenham*

Contents

Introduction

God is Man's response to a legacy of evolutionary discontent. The faculty of conceptual thought that has raised Man above all other forms of animal life was achieved only at the cost of a divided and tormented mind. Some twenty-five million years ago Man's primate ancestors embarked on a hazardous road that would lead one day to his controlling the evolutionary process itself, and thus achieving the means of engineering his own extinction. It would give him the ability to colonise other planets in his galaxy, and to destroy his own. It would produce from his ranks the genius and the schizophrenic, and lead his dreamers to the gates of heaven and hell. Man's response to that awful burden of self-determination was to create for himself a god and to still his self-doubts in the solace of religion.

To understand the origins of this concept we must briefly survey the story of Man's evolution from the beginning of life on this planet to the emergence of *Homo sapiens*, 'knowing Man'. For, after all, what we know of God, or think we know, must be an expression of our own humanity, gained from experience, first-hand and inherited. Whether such a divine father-figure exists in reality, or, if he does, can communicate with Man and really offer him guidance and consolation, can only be a matter for philosophic speculation; it is not capable of scientific demonstration. What is certain is that the various faiths and practices of mankind show certain common characteristics that spring from our basic humanity and are a product of our evolutionary development.

In the chapters that follow, we shall try to relate such concepts to bio-psychological factors in Man's peculiar evolutionary history. His needs, frustrations and fears, he projected into his relationships with the gods, and found in religion a means of reliving his emotional stresses and, later, of constructing a philosophical framework that could temporarily satisfy his growing curiosity about himself and the natural world. His imagination played upon such intellectual speculations and expressed them in everyday terms, in saga, song, and story, to form the stuff of mythology. Its making has been a cumulative process, and many of its underlying themes tend to become lost in the colourful pageant of heroic exploits that dazzle the eye and entrance the ear of the listener. Much of the work of the modern mythologist is directed towards disentangling and identifying the themes that engaged so much of early Man's thinking, in order to gain an insight into his intellectual awakening. From mythology's rich heritage we may recognise landmarks in the development of Man's religious ideas and here and there catch a glimpse of his lost gods.

Gods disappear from history because they are no longer required. Man created them for specific purposes in particular circumstances; when conditions change, social or ecological, gods become outdated and are superseded by more effective deities, imported usually from alien cosmologies by merchants and invaders. But human nature is more deeply rooted, and Man's emotional needs are fundamentally similar whatever the time or place. The new gods must therefore speak to the same inadequacies of Man in his unequal struggle against the environment, and their worship must somehow satisfy that deep longing in the human heart for peace of mind and assurance for the future. In this sense the deist is right to argue that there is but one God with many faces.

The divisiveness in religious loyalties has been disastrous for humanity, as we know too well. Wars fought to assert the claims to supremacy of rival theological systems, or even of differing ways of serving the same deity, have been among the most ruthless and bitter. In so individual a matter of a man's relationship with his god, it is not surprising that there should be great differences among the creeds and rituals of people living in widely different environments. Such variations will be very largely the product of local needs and customs, and it is in the nature of a system that seeks to establish a long continuity of relationship between a people and its deity that religious thought is essentially conservative; innovations are viewed with suspicion and, where reluctantly accepted under political or ecological pressures, must be seen to have roots deeply set in the soil of local tradition. Thus regional and ethnic variations of common religious themes assume an importance in the eyes of their adherents that tend to obscure more basic concepts shared with alien faiths.

In a rapidly shrinking world and ever closer interdependence of ethnic and political groups, there is no room for religious intolerance. The recent interest in some form of religious ecumenism is but one aspect of a growing awareness of the need to reappraise Man's common concerns and heritage. If it is too much at this stage of our intellectual development to ask that some less emotional motivation should determine our understanding of the world and human destiny, we should at least appreciate that our search for a god stems from a discontent that is part of our common genetic background. This is the theme of our book.

1

God is Twenty-five Million Years Old

For more than half of its existence, this planet was in no condition to support life. Then, about two thousand million years ago, a combination of climatic and environmental circumstances allowed the formation of a new and wonderful molecular structure that was able not only to reproduce itself, but to store and pass on to its offspring a chemical blueprint that determined its nature and function. Self-regenerating and self-duplicating life had been born. However, since no copying process in nature is entirely exact, once every so often the transmitted code varies slightly from its pattern. The result is a mutation, making the progeny in some way different from its parents. The change might be for the good, perhaps helping the offspring to adapt more readily to a change in environment, or for worse, depriving it of some faculty and thus threatening the strain with extinction. If the new organism is a success it will proliferate at the expense of less-favoured neighbours, and its novel, advantageous features will be transmitted by the revised blueprint to subsequent generations.

These are the mechanics of the Darwinian principle of evolution by natural selection. There is no ordered advancement here, no steady, inevitable rise to perfection, least of all, as far as one can see, any master-planning in the long and wasteful process. But the possibility of variation does at least make progress possible. Were the copying system to be entirely flawless, no change could ever occur and the primeval soup would have continued to produce identical molecules reproducing themselves *ad infinitum* to nobody's interest save their own. As it is, within each population of living cells there will be a number of mutants that have the capability of responding to environmental change that might otherwise have threatened the existence of the whole species. All the remaining cells within that group might perish, but the few that have embodied the fortuitous change at the right time will survive and eventually replenish the strain.

Measured in human terms the process must seem interminably long and inordinately wasteful. Nevertheless, once reproductive life had begun, with this built-in capacity for self-variation, the rate of development could increase beyond anything that might have been achieved in the previous stage of random atom collisions. Within only hundreds of millions of years the surface of the planet was covered with living creatures, bacteria, viruses, algae, and, later, with fish, plants, amphibia, reptiles, birds, and mammals. Then, some sixty-five million years ago, there appeared the first prosimian ('pre-monkey') ancestors of our lemurs, lorises, and tarsiers. Today we know some fifty-odd species of these animals, some of which do not appear to have varied from their original course of development. The most conservative are the eighteen kinds of tree-shrew that inhabit the warmer parts of southern Asia. These highly-developed, squirrel-like creatures have teeth that suit their insect- and fruit-eating habits and betray their mammalian ancestry. We may see in the tree-shrew something very close to the first primate, the decisive step towards monkeys, apes, and Man himself. With *Homo sapiens* the whole process of evolution entered a new, faster, and infinitely more exciting and dangerous phase.

The old order of progress, by random mutations reacting with changes in environment, was superseded. Man does not depend on genetic mutation for his adaptation and survival. Thanks to his facility for conceptual thought, symbolic language and memory, he can pass on accumulated experience to his progeny by cultural means. His body is, of course, not immune to genetic variations; he is still largely the product of his parents, physically and mentally, but he can use his gift of imagination and foresight to assess and counter the difficulties that beset him at any one time, taking the necessary steps to forestall dangers that might threaten him in the future. He can challenge his environment, not wait for some rearrangement of his genetic chemistry to adapt his species to a change of conditions. He has invented fire to supplement his limited means of self-defence against predatory animals. He has devised means of hunting other creatures not only for food, but to use their skins to cover the nakedness that would otherwise have restricted his movement to warmer climes.

But for the branching-off of the line that produced the genus *Homo,* we need to go back to a time when a large part of the surface of our planet was covered with huge areas of unbroken forest. From the beginning of the age of mammals, rising temperatures had brought with them this exuberance of vegetation, and we owe much of our most important physical and psychological inheritance to the forest-life of our ancestors.

At first, the Prosimians lived on the ground, but later their predators, particularly the rodents, drove them to take refuge in the trees. If our ability to detect scent changes is now virtually non-existent when compared with, say, that of a dog, we must blame those ancient enemies that drove our forebears aloft. If now we lack long snouts, and our eyes are in front of our faces instead of at the side, we can thank our branch-leaping ancestors for their demand for sharp, stereoscopic vision to judge distance accurately. If we now have flattened fingernails instead of claws like the squirrel, and long fingers with opposable thumbs that enable us to grip objects, we can attribute our manipulative skills to the need to grasp branches. Even more important, the new tempo of arboreal locomotion, quick reflex action, instantaneous eye and muscle co-ordination, demanded a much more elaborate brain. The cerebral cortex that began as a pin-head of cells on the brain surface of the first amphibians, now expanded to cover the walnut-sized prosimian brain as a fine grey skin of millions of cells.

Tree-life proved a success. Once the Prosimians had adapted sufficiently to cope with their new and fast-moving environment, they could multiply in safety and spread to dominate the forests of the world for millions of years. But evolution cannot be static. Larger and more specialised tree-dwellers emerged, and monkeys began to oust their predecessors. Their fingers developed even more sensitive touch and a greater mobility which not only enabled them to grab hold of passing branches more efficiently, but to grasp and manipulate objects, from large sticks to wield as weapons to the smallest seeds and insects for food. The world of the primate became increasingly resolved into 'me and 'it', subject and object. This first philosophical principle, the beginning of Man's self-consciousness, was of vital importance in the psychological development of our species.

The monkeys were in time joined by other primates, larger in size and in some ways more adaptable. Their larger bodies and heavier weight gave them an advantage in the constant battle against predators, but at the cost of diminished agility in the trees. However, their comparative invulnerability meant that they could also return in safety to the ground, and this freedom of habitat gave them a wider choice of foraging territory. Furthermore, with their inherited advantages of a well-defined stereoscopic vision, a good hand for grasping, and a fine brain capable of almost infinite development, this promising creature was equipped for a more adventurous life than anything the pampering forest could offer, with its ever-available food supply. What was required now was a new incentive to encourage the development of potential generated by this combination of faculties, and this was provided by a radical change in the planet's surface structure.

Some twenty-five million years ago the forests were being split asunder to make room for increasing areas of grassland. The earth's crust had buckled and pushed up sediment deposits from the beds of the primeval seas into great mountain chains, like the Alps and Himalayas. Temperatures fell, and violent rains eroded the mountain slopes. In their lee spread the savannahs, penetrated by long fingers of peninsula forests. It was here, at the edges of these plains, against a backcloth of the forests that had been the home and refuge of their predecessors, that Man's remote ancestors embarked on their great adventures in open country. This was to be the stage for the evolutionary drama that would challenge their resourcefulness and stimulate their rise to precedence over all other creatures. This was, in effect, the birthplace of Man and his religion.

2

Gentlemen, Be Upstanding

Scholars are generally agreed that we so-called hominids ('Sons of Man') may trace our descent, along with such higher primates as chimpanzees, gorillas, and orang utans, to a family of early apes called *Dryopithecinae* ('Tree-apes'), whose African type-specimen is known as Proconsul (after a chimp in the London zoo). He was little bigger than a gibbon, and, despite his generic name, spent only part of his time swinging in the trees; his limbs show that he was also equipped for life on the ground. Unfortunately, for almost all of the twenty-five million years that have elapsed since his time, the hominid line is uncertainly represented in the fossil record; indeed, we are the only primate family that lacks an incontestably accepted ancestor living before the Ice Age. Happily the apes are better served, and we may reasonably judge our likely progress through this long, uncharted span of time by reference to that family, the so-called *Pongidae.* We can at least know for certain that we are related to the apes, however distantly, by comparing general skeleton structures, muscular anatomy, and the arrangement of the visceral organs. Furthermore, comparative anti-serum tests show that of that family our closest affinity is with the gorillas and chimpanzees, rather than monkeys and gibbons. In fact, the last-named animal may well be able to trace its distinctive line of descent from about the same time as Proconsul, a point of interest to us since its family life has some resemblance to our own.

We can be sure that there was no single, undeviating progression from pre-human ape to *Homo sapiens.* There must have been many dead ends, petering out through local circumstances, or allowing precedence to some more adaptable species moving on to the scene from elsewhere. It is not inconceivable that the evolution of Man followed similar paths simultaneously in different parts of the world, although from the evidence so far available it does seem that Africa was the centre of the most significant advances. It is from that continent, and particularly from east and south, that the majority of the earliest hominid fossils have come, recording particularly that developed species of pre-Man known as *Australopithecus*, 'Southern Ape'. But by this time we have entered upon the most recent geological epoch of this planet, the Ice Age, or Pleistocene, beginning, it is variously estimated, between three and one million years ago, and ending, if, indeed, it has ended, around 8300 BC. During that time, successive sheets of ice, thousands of feet thick, covered a large part of the northern hemisphere. The first of these glaciations, the Early or Lower Pleistocene, saw the appearance of *Australopithecus*. This hominid stood at the very threshold of true manhood. He was small in stature, less than five feet tall and weighing around 100 pounds. His head was chinless, with massive jaws, strongly defined brow ridges, and a sloping forehead. His teeth were characteristically hominid in their arrangement on a rounded arcade, and in the comparatively small size of the canines.

But the most striking difference from his simian relatives was in the way he walked in a more erect posture, on two feet. He was no longer committed to life in the trees, and this is a natural consequence of the movement begun millions of years earlier, when his ancestors began to leave the shelter of the forests and ventured forth upon the neighbouring plains. *Australopithecus* no longer had the specialised development of limbs and shoulders necessary for swinging from branches, and, when he walked, it was not with the forward-bending stance of the ape. His pelvis shows without doubt that he walked erect, for it has become a basin to contain the viscera, rather than, as previously, a frame from which to hang them.

This erect posture probably had more effect on the technological, social, and psychological progress of Man's evolution than any other single feature. But whatever its primary cause, walking on two feet, or bipedalism, as it is called, was not the result of any marked increase in hominid intelligence, for the brain of *Australopithecus* was still no larger than the ape's, about a third that of *Homo sapiens.* An erect stance would certainly give the early hominid several advantages, but again it was not the inevitable result of his descent from the trees. Other primates, such as the baboon, can live in the trees and yet move around quite satisfactorily on the ground using all four limbs. Certainly, to be able to stand upright amid the tall grasses of the savannah offers considerable advantages in reconnoitring, but it has the drawback of making the animal itself more conspicuous.

Much more significant is the freeing of the forelimbs that bipedalism makes possible. The arms can then be used for gathering and carrying, and in a meat-eating situation this faculty would have been of some importance. Even a modest kill would have given the hominid more food than he could consume on the spot at one sitting, and if, by then, spoil-sharing was already customary among carnivores, it might well have been necessary to transport the carcase to a safe retreat. Carrying it in the arms would certainly have been preferable to dragging it any distance.

But again, food-sharing alone hardly seems a strong enough stimulus to the selection of the biped over his four-footed cousin, who is often quite capable of carrying fruits some yards to a refuge. More important by far is the use of hands to fashion and wield instruments for work or war, be they no more complicated than large sticks or defoliated branches for digging or waving aloft. Where such 'arm-extensions' are used for the purpose of asserting authority over, say, a territory or mate, they act in the manner of aggrandisement techniques adopted by lesser animals and birds to frighten off competitors. In the case of apes, the gesture is rarely taken the lengths of actually striking the opponent, but, like the baring of canine teeth and other forms of facial display, it merely serves as a warning. Sometimes, indeed, waving a branch aloft has no more than a ritualistic quality in times of excitement, that has nothing at all to do with territorial encroachment or personal assault.

It is true that the use of hands for manipulating simple tools is not confined to hominids. Chimpanzees have been observed drawing termites from their mounds by probing the hardened earth with neatly trimmed and shortened sticks. This fairly delicate operation requires considerable foresight, since the animal will often prepare the implement before he has located the hillocks, which are ripe for plundering only at certain restricted seasons before the onset of the rains. It is then that the termites prepare for their own breakout by drilling through the underside of the concrete-like shell of their mounds to within a fraction of an inch of the surface.

But then, if such intelligent and purposeful tool-using were already within the capabilities of the pre-hominid primate, any further adaptation likely to improve this valuable facility would tend to encourage the selection of a biped with forelimbs available for further specialisation. As with most evolutionary changes, there would have been cross-fertilisation between use and adaptation. In this case it resulted in an improvement in the gripping abilities of the hand and digital control as opportunities for ever more sophisticated tool-devising presented themselves. And as the forelimbs became more and more suitable to these ends, so their aptitude as aids to locomotion would increase and the bonus advantages of an erect posture would play their part in favouring the biped.

The skeletal changes involved in standing erect and

running on two feet posed new problems, however. The basin-like form of the adapted pelvis is well suited for holding the viscera, but it has also to allow for the passage of urinary, alimentary, and reproductive ducts. Its bony floor cannot therefore be continuous, and the muscular and fascial diaphragm that closes the necessary gap is itself perforated and thus to some extent weakened. There is a constant pressure on the pelvic diaphragm in the erect attitude while standing still, and this increases with the slightest movement of the arms. Bending down to pick up a heavy object raises that pressure fivefold, and if the movement is violent or sudden, it can rise tenfold. There will thus always be a tendency for organs to slide out or prolapse from the pelvis, or to seek out the weakest spots and protrude from the opening. With all this, the maternal pelvis must allow for the passage of a large-headed baby without permanently disarranging the mother's anatomy or damaging the infant.

This large-headedness is a distinguishing feature of the developing hominid. *Australopithecus*'s brain was still small by human standards, but the next stage in our evolution brought a sudden increase in brain size, and with it a larger capacity for rational thought and controlled action. In the Mid-Pleistocene period, usually put at about half-a-million years ago, the 'Southern apes' had to face the challenge of a subhuman primate called *Homo erectus*. We have no sure means of knowing whether he evolved directly out of *Australopithecus*, or whether they both represent offshoots from some hitherto unidentified common stock. But certainly from that time the days of *Australopithecus* were numbered, for, however large and robust he might grow, he could not match the brain-power and low cunning of the more evolved creature. His brain capacity was nearly double that of his predecessor, reaching even into the lower ranges of *Homo sapiens*.

Not that physical size alone is a true measure of the

brain's reasoning capacity, or women would inevitably be less intelligent than men. A proportion of any increase in brain-size is related to growth in overall body-weight. In Man this amounts to about ten or twelve per cent; whether big or small, male or female, *Homo sapiens* needs a certain number of neurones and their connecting fibres to let him act in a co-ordinated, rational, 'human' way. If a specimen of *Homo erectus*, of around modern body-weight, had a cranial capacity of two-thirds that of a human, only eighty-two per cent of his brain's mass could be reckoned as contributing to his powers of reasoning. So even the meanest human brain has a greater potential for intelligent thought than was possesed by the best-endowed *Homo erectus*.

Again, it is not so much the overall weight of the brain that determines intelligence, as its construction. The hemispheres of the brain are divided into lobes whose surfaces are covered with the cortex, a wrinkled skin of grey matter containing the all-important neurones. Lobes can differ in size among individuals and races, and in the complexity and depths of the folds offered as surface areas for the spread of grey matter.

The sharp increase in the size and complexity of the brain that occurred among hominids of the Ice Age was achieved through the same wasteful, hit-or-miss process of natural selection that characterises evolution generally. The difference lay in the speed of advance displayed by the developing organism as it responded to a rapidly changing cultural and ecological scene. Within a million years the hominid had doubled the size of his brain without any marked increase in bodysize.

We have already seen how, all those many millions of years before, the early primates responded to their three-dimensional arboreal environment by developing a more complex nervous system through proliferation of cerebral grey matter. The primitive 'smell-brain' needed to be augmented, and to some extent superseded, by a new capability to cope with the flood of visual information offered by the animal's much improved optical apparatus. This expansion of the cortex took place at the back of the head, while new areas at its sides developed to deal with ever-increasing demands for more sensitive and instantaneous responses from and to the fingers.

Now the branch-swinging primate's successor needed to extend his brain's capability into areas of control and deliberation that went far beyond automatic responses to outward stimuli. To survive and proliferate, he must overcome rivals who could hunt slow game, hurl stones, and even fashion simple stone tools and weapons, as well as he could himself. *Homo erectus* must prove himself superior by seeking out and preying upon larger and swifter animals, better equipped with tooth and claw, whose tracking down and ensnaring required careful planning, mutual collaboration, systems of food-sharing and conservation, acceptance of leadership, provision for defence of the home base during extended hunting trips, protection against the elements in the open country by night and day. Archaeology shows how well this pre-Man succeeded: his skeleton tells us what manner of a creature he was, the remains of his camps indicate the nature of his prey, and the weapons and tools he used to kill and prepare their flesh. Burnt embers declare his greatest cultural achievement, the invention of fire to defend his camps, to warm his body, and to provide a focus of social intercourse. *Australopithecus* stayed around a while longer, perhaps contributing in some measure to a common gene pool, but in the end he could not compete with this superior creature and died out, a victim to the brainpower of Man's immediate predecessor.

However, as we saw, the evolution of a bigger-brained primate brought its attendant anatomical difficulties. There is a limit to the capability of the hominid maternal pelvis to allow passage to a big-headed baby; when further cranial expansion is required it must occur outside the womb. So while, for example, rhesus monkey offspring are born with brains already three-quarters their adult size, those of *Homo erectus* had probably completed only a third of their optimum growth; the remainder of the process had to take place in the hostile world outside the mother. Now at least she could hold and protect her babies with forelimbs freed from ambulatory functions, since she could move around on two feet. And hold the baby she must, for the small creature had by now lost the ability enjoyed by the young of lower orders of primates to grip their mothers' fur with their feet. They had to be born mature enough to cling on and move with the pack.

Once through the pelvic canal, the hominid infant could develop a large cranium and expand the cerebral lobes within. But this takes time. The human baby's brain at birth has only reached twenty-four per cent of its adult mass, at three years it has attained eighty-two per cent, and even at ten, just before puberty, there is another five per cent to go to maturity. During those early years the hominid child, to judge from human standards, had much to learn and was at continual risk. The demands it made upon its parents, and particularly its mother, during its uniquely extended childhood and adolescence brought their own social and domestic problems, as we shall see. But no less burdensome are the anatomical needs of this expensive organ. Indeed, its demands on the rest of the hominid organism are so great and persistent as would surely have condemned the absurdly complex apparatus to an early end as one of nature's more bizarre experiments had not selective pressures insisted on making increasing intelligence a condition of survival.

For one thing, the brain and large skull that contains it are too heavy for the rest of the body and need undue support from bones, tendons, and muscles in the neck, trunk and legs. It is also far too sensitive to temperature variations for an organ so exposed to the elements. Only the viscera are so intolerant, and they are far better protected with fleshy parts. The brain's thermal range is controlled within its fine limits by various external means like head-hair, suitably thick, thin, straight, or curly, to match the prevailing climate, and more vitally by a copious blood supply. To feed and regulate this cerebral liability monopolises twelve per cent of the body's available blood flow although it comprises only two per cent of the body's bulk. And, as sufferers from heart condition know too well, even a momentary interruption in blood supplies is very swiftly and peremptorily punished.

To recapitulate: after some two billion years of evolution by natural selection, nature had produced in *Homo erectus* a primate that could use his forelimbs to make and use stone tools, create fire when he wanted it, invent speech, and in general achieve his ends by cunning, collaboration, and dogged perseverance. His greatest asset was a growing intelligence through a complex nervous system that was already making disproportionate demands upon his bodily resources. Physically he was running into trouble. By balancing his ungainly body on two feet he had condemned his females to the pains of parturition and his males to backache. He had sacrificed a round-the-clock perceptiveness through smell and hearing for an over-dependence on daylight and unimpaired vision, and he had compelled a herbivoral digestive apparatus to adapt to a meat diet. Ecologically he had begun to alienate himself from the rest of the animal world, and sexually he was already demanding of the reproductive urge a companionate function that could not be confined to mere hours or days of oestral receptivity. In fact, the evolutionary advances that had brought the primate to the verge of manhood contained within them the germs of self-destruction, and along with his growing intelligence came the appreciation of his own inadequacy and insecurity, an essential element of religious faith.

3

Family Life

The primates are social animals. The way they associate and the precise relationship between members of each group varies considerably with the species. But in general, monkeys and apes live in close proximity to others of their kind and their individual well-being depends upon their relations with one another. The defensive cohesiveness of the group, for instance, is of special importance to a species facing constant threats from predators. This kind of recurrent danger needs a strong disciplinary organisation based upon a rigid dominance hierarchy and chain of command. Every animal must be aware of its position in society and its defensive role. The leadership may normally only be challenged when the dominant male can no longer command the respect of his inferiors and thus becomes a menace to the welfare of the group.

We can see just such an authoritarian organisation, for example, among the Japanese Macaque monkeys *(Macaca tuscata)*. In each colony there is a gang of dominant males that operate as an oligarchy. The whole group circulates around them like an enormous, shared harem. When they move from one feeding-place to another, a party of young males goes in front, followed by a cluster of females, infants, and babies, accompanied by the dominant males. The rearguard is brought up by another group of young warriors. On reaching the new feeding-ground, the leaders and the females with their young remain in the centre, while the young males encircle them in a protective ring. Only when the leaders have finished feeding may the young bloods move in to begin eating. It is then apparent to the observer that these also have their social 'pecking-order' and must know and keep their places in relation to one another.

The leaders never quarrel among themselves at the feeding-site; each knows his own place in the hierarchy and for the time being, at least, accepts the position. They combine to keep order also among the females and juveniles, and they check any intrusion by ambitious guards on the periphery. The outer ring in turn watches for incursions from solitary males operating outside the group, who might otherwise enter the outskirts during feeding periods and gather a few females in order to form an independent colony.

The mating habits of the macaque monkeys are similarly organised on a hierarchical basis. Non-human female primates are receptive only during periods of 'heat', or oestrus. This may be only for a few days in each month, and will not occur at all during lactation and pregnancy. When the Japanese Macaque comes into heat she consorts regularly with one of the dominant males, staying for the period of her oestrus close to her chosen mate. There is no particular competition for her favours since there are more than enough females to go round. Some, indeed, may sidle off and establish illicit relationships with the normally non-participating young bachelors on the fringe, taking care to avoid being caught by the dominant males.

A similar oligarchical organisation exists among the East African baboons, There, too, the 'top brass' rule the whole group in a strict order of rank, and combine to counter threats from outside the community. The female baboon is receptive for about a week in every month, and from the very beginning of oestrus she makes advances to the males. During the first few days she will seek the favours of mere subordinates and older juveniles. At this stage there is less chance of her conceiving, and it is only in the last days of heat, when she is properly fertile, that she becomes irresistible to the dominant males. Then she establishes a brief but intense sexual relationship with one of the bosses, and this may last from one or two hours to several days. Genetically, this selective mechanism has the advantage of bringing the female into contact with a partner offering the greatest breeding potential only when she can best profit from his attention; the resulting offspring will thus maintain the strain at its optimum. But at the same time, her sexual availability from the beginning of oestrus when she is least fertile, means that less favoured males are offered some outlet for their libidinous energies. This avoids a dangerous build-up of sexual energy into the kind of stress situation which might result from prolonged celibacy. We shall have occasion to refer to this problem later.

In an open habitat fraught with danger from predatory enemies, survival depends upon the maintenance of rigid discipline within the community, and puts a premium on selective breeding. But in the relative security of the forests, this kind of ruthless tyranny in social relationships is unnecessary, and some more relaxed attitude prevails between group members. Among such arboreal monkeys as the Indian langur, for instance, baboon-type dominance is noticeably absent. When a female is in heat, she will offer herself to any male available, whatever his social standing. Even during copulation there is a relaxed atmosphere surrounding the pair that is far removed from the jealous possessiveness shown by a baboon leader exercising his mating prerogative. The langur couple may be surrounded by a heckling, jostling group of male onlookers and yet remain remarkably unperturbed.

Further up the primate scale, chimpanzees and gorillas demonstrate even greater social harmony. Dominance behaviour among chimps is minimal, although the differing social status of young and old, inexperienced and mature, male and female, is clearly recognised. There are, however, no permanent leaders of such groups, and the dominant males exercise no exclusive rights over oestral females. Jane Van Lawick

Goodall, the British naturalist, has observed seven males, including an adolescent, copulate in succession with one female and yet demonstrate no aggression towards one another. One aged female, whom she named Flo, seemed particularly well-endowed with sex-appeal and in times of heat was followed everywhere by a large male retinue. During one oestral session, Jane Goodall saw an unusual relationship develop between Flo and one of her male followers named Rodolf. It seems to have come close to the kind of permanent pair-bonding relationship that is characteristic of the next stage in sexual relationships:

> He walked everywhere just beside or behind her, he stopped when she stopped, he slept in the nest closest to hers. And it was to Rodolf that Flo hurried when she was hurt or frightened during those weeks and he would lay his hand reassuringly on her, or, sometimes, put one arm around her. Yet he did not protest in any way when other males mated with Flo . . .
>
> Rodolf showed none of the bullying aggressive behaviour towards Flo which characterised the relationship of Leakey [another male chimpanzee in the group] and the others to the females of their choice. . . . Rodolf remained with Flo and her family for the two weeks after her swelling had vanished.

Dr Goodall adds:

> It is, of course, fruitless to speculate as to the sort of heterosexual relationships which might develop if chimpanzee physiology were different: if, for example, Flo had been able to offer Rodolf continuing sexual satisfaction, if the family reproductive cycle of the chimp were the same as that of the human. The fact remains that female chimpanzees have evolved in such a way that they are only sexually receptive to males for a mere ten days per month; provided, that is, that they are neither pregnant nor lactating which, in older females, means that they may be denied sexual activity for up to five years. . . . (*In the Shadow of Man*, 1974, p. 189).

Somewhere along the evolutionary path this radical alteration in primate sexuality occurred. It became necessary for the development of permanent pair-bond relationships for sex to mean far more than a mere device for fertilising the female; it had to be extended into a means for drawing individuals together and holding them until at least their offspring had survived their uniquely prolonged infancy. The male needed to be continually attracted to his mate, not merely for the few hectic days around her period of ovulation. The vulnerable infants could no longer be left to fend for themselves whilst their mothers indulged in a frantic orgy of sexual gratification during their oestrus. Doubtless this increase in sexual attractiveness was gradual; we saw above how it allows the female baboon a chance to relieve the libidinous energies of young males not yet genetically ready to father first-ranking children. Here already is the first move towards separating the reproductive and communicatory functions of sex. As mating became a means of continual communication between the partners, the span of female receptiveness would have been broadened, her erogenous zones extended, and mutual grooming would have become less concerned with cleaning each other's fur and more with expressing affection, and, as in human 'petting', with sexual arousal.

As far as social grouping is concerned, it is the small, highly mobile gibbon which comes closest among the apes to the pattern of the human family. The species may have branched off the common ape stock very early on, preferring to remain in the trees and develop high-speed arboreal locomotion rather than grow large and ponderous on the ground. The male gibbon accompanies a single female and two or three offspring of different ages. The male and female are of equal status in matters of leading, co-ordinating, and guarding the group, and they can be equally aggressive, biting and clawing when the need arises. The families maintain a strict territorial discipline, and when the male adolescents grow old enough to present a challenge to their father's authority, they are driven away to establish new territories of their own.

Physically closer to Man, the gorilla moves around more widely through less clearly demarcated territories, carrying or leading his young. But gorilla paterfamilias is less possessive than the gibbon; he allows a few unrelated males to accompany his family and even to take their turn with an oestral female. Only when they make some overt attempt to usurp the father's authority, does the older silverback see them off. At times two families will join forces, but the association is only temporary, and before long they will separate and go their various ways.

Within such small social groups as the family unit, the father has a much more positive role to play in the rearing of the young. The baboon baby is entirely the responsibility of the mother who, during its short but intensive period of dependence, offers it comfort and security as well as food. Soon it will leave her to play with other infants and start preparing for enrolment in the ranks of aspirants to the dominating hierarchy. The gorilla father, on the other hand, shares the mother's responsibility for the training of the young during its time of helplessness which, as we saw, becomes progressively longer with the evolution of the higher primates. More and more time is required outside the womb for the infant to learn to fend for itself and to develop the potentialities of his comparatively large brain, and the gorilla father is continually on hand to contribute to this learning experience.

In looking across at these forms of family and social grouping among living primates, we may recognise elements in each reflecting the human situation. It is true that no species of the larger apes adequately represents Man's non-oestral pair-bonding arrangement for the care of the newly-born, or approaches the human potential for creative thought. Nevertheless, with care it is possible to supplement the sparse fossil and archaeological information on the social behaviour of our forebears with observations of our primate cousins in the wild.

As far as numbers are concerned, it is reasonable to assume that small groups of hominids would have stood a better chance of survival in times of drought and widely dispersed food supplies than large populations foraging together. The African Australopithecines probably lived in communities of no more than twenty or thirty, grouped around home bases consisting of simple stone windbreaks. If, in times of extreme heat or cold, they sought out caves or overhanging cliffs for shelter, it would probably be only in daytime, for the caves were also the lairs of more efficient killers, and, until the invention of fire, the hominids would have fared better in the open.

The hazardous nature of the Australopithecines' life in the savannah, burdened as they were by now with particularly vulnerable females and offspring demanding constant vigilance and protection, meant that each group of individuals must have been organised into some kind of cohesive unit for defence. This in turn implies the establishment of a hierarchy based upon division of labour and responsibility. The older males, by virtue of their superior strength and mobility, must have provided the first line of defence and have been individually responsible for the welfare of each family. The prime role of the females would have been dictated for them by the overriding demands of motherhood, although, in this pre-hunting situation, both sexes would have been equally adept at food collection, in grubbing for roots and capturing slow-game.

More important for our studies are the psychological consequences of the continuous presence within each family group of a single dominant male, on the assumed lines of a gibbon-gorilla type of paternalism. This must have given rise to a number of potential areas of stress between parents and their young, especially between the father and his male offspring. The infant would have found himself torn between wanting to keep close to his mother, as the prime source of food and comfort, and having to avoid provoking his father into a display of jealous hostility that could end by the youngster being driven from the family group. All the evidence of primate behaviour suggests that the presence of another male within such a closely-knit social group would have appeared to the adult as an actual or potential threat to his authority and sexual rights. For whether or not the father would consciously consider an infant a serious contender for his mate's attentions, the fact is that even in infancy a young primate displays in his well-developed external genitalia signals that could be read by a confronting male as a challenge necessitating a counter-display of aggression.

The close connection between male sexuality and aggression among mammals is well established. The copulatory act is itself a form of aggression: the male mounts and penetrates his partner's body with his own. The female's role is essentially submissive: she presents her genitals to the male in the way that best permits the entry of his penis. Among the primates, these sexually-orientated attitudes came to be used in non-copulatory situations to express aggression and submission generally (see below, Chapter Five). Thus monkeys and apes of either sex will seek to placate a potential enemy by 'presenting', crouching with raised rump directed towards the other party, who responds by 'mounting', even where no copulation is intended or, indeed, in the case of two females, even possible. Among juvenile monkeys this custom is copied although neither participant may be physically capable of achieving full copulation.

The male signals his dominance by erecting his penis, often brilliantly coloured to enhance the effectiveness of the gesture. Among some monkeys, a male on the edge of the group will hold outsiders at bay by sitting on its haunches, legs apart, and displaying a fully erect penis, even motivating it repeatedly to strike his stomach. The little squirrel monkey uses his 'status symbol' not merely as a general warning-sign to passersby, but as a direct threat towards an inferior. He goes up close and obtrusively erects his penis in the other's face.

The *Australopithecus* paterfamilias is thus confronted within his family circle with what appears to be a threat to this supremacy. If he does not immediately respond to the danger signals and see the intruder off, it can only be that some other, more powerful factor is overriding his natural inclinations. Even if, at this early stage in hominid development, we should hesitate to ascribe such restraint to pure reason, we are justified in recognising here the beginnings of rational self-control and the dawn of an awareness of social responsibility. In the interests of the common good, the primate has learnt to stay his hand, to hesitate before yielding to the prompting of his instincts, and to consider an alternative line of action.

When the hominid thus responds consciously to the constrictive demands of life within a closely-knit family group, evolution has entered a new phase. Increasingly he will learn to co-operate with his fellows for the well-being of the community, and, as he crosses the threshold of reason, his culture will enable him to control his own environment and thus his own development. Rationality will begin to moderate the random forces of mutation in the evolutionary process.

That the Australopithecine father did learn to live with junior, and junior to behave circumspectly within the family circle, is proved by the survival of the species for hundreds of thousands of years. But the achievement was bought dearly. The kind of stress involved in this primitive father-son relationship has been seen by some as the ultimate source of that anxiety state known as the 'Oedipus complex'.

The first recognition and clinical description of this condition we owe to the Viennese psychologist Sigmund Freud. It seemed to him that many of his neurotically disturbed male patients owed much of their trouble to anxieties originating far back in childhood. Between the ages of four and six, they shared a common experience that revealed itself under deep psychoanalysis as a strange preoccupation with their own genitals and an overwhelming fear that their love for their mother would incur their father's retribution. They even imagined that he would take his revenge by castrating them. For it was evident that the affection shown by Freud's patients for their mothers had been frankly sexual and incestuous, and seemed to Freud to reflect in real life the dramatic circumstances portrayed in the classical myth of Oedipus, who unwittingly killed his own father and married his own mother. On learning the truth, and overcome with guilt, Oedipus blinded, or castrated, himself in expiation.

Freud believed that if his patients' anxieties were not resolved early on in childhood, the infantile tensions of divided love and loyalties, and their irrational fears of parental punishment, might exert a crippling influence upon normal sexual relationships in later life. Heterosexual encounters would be avoided, and the sex-drive, or libido, would be given unnatural outlets through homosexuality, fetish cults, or other deviant practices. The sense of guilt could disturb the patient's relationships with other people throughout his life.

Freud's basic assumptions, methods, and validity of his patients' revelations under psychoanalysis have all been brought seriously into question, particularly of recent years. Nevertheless, the neurotic symptoms with which the master tried to deal are real enough, and it may well be that many of our modern sexual neuroses can be traced to this formative period in hominid psychological development. Our ancestors were trying to move away from a large baboon-like pack grouping into a smaller, family-based arrangement of living. The adult male had become an integral part of the family circle, continually attracted sexually to his mate, and sharing in the upbringing of their offspring. He had to be able to assert his authority in times of danger, and yet to relax his jealous aggressiveness in the interests of domestic harmony and the rearing of his young. Small wonder if this change in a long-established behavioural pattern at such a crucial time in hominid development should have left its mark in human psychology.

Freud suggested that his 'Oedipus complex' was not only one of the most important sources of obsessional guilt among neurotics, but that Man may have acquired his sense of guilt generally from this deep-seated trauma. He even saw it as the prime source of religion and morality. There is, of course, far more to religion than a sense of guilt, but we have to agree that the sources of Man's 'divine discontent' are as deep in the human psyche as the peculiar evolutionary circumstances that have produced in *Homo sapiens* our strangely ambivalent attitudes to parental love and human sexuality. For what religious Man came eventually to think of as 'conscience' is simply the faculty that enabled his hominid ancestors to inhibit their programmed responses to stimuli in the interests of some longer-term advantage; 'guilt' is the unease that accompanies and sometimes motivates that control; and God is the idealistic projection of the conscience in moral terms. Through his religions Man both dramatises the conflict and seeks its resolution. Unhappily for our peace of mind, that unease is an integral part of human nature: the spur that was necessary to drive the primate into intelligent Manhood remains with us as the energy that motivates our conscious minds to ordered thinking.

4

Nimrod

> Cush became the father of Nimrod; he was the first on earth to be a mighty man. He was a mighty hunter before the Lord; therefore it is said, 'Like Nimrod a mighty hunter before the Lord'.
>
> (*Genesis* 10:8–9)

When Man's remote ancestors developed a taste for meat to supplement their largely vegetarian diet, they set in train a whole series of physical, psychological, and social changes which crucially affected the development of *Homo sapiens*. Keen, stereoscopic vision the primate already had, a legacy of his move from the forest floor to the trees. Now he would need to pit his wits and body against the animals of the plain, fleeter of foot, and already long adapted to the crafts of stalking prey and ambush.

Physically he grew larger, and joined that select band of big mammals who demand a disproportionately greater expanse of territory per head than is justified on grounds of individual bulk. A large animal needs more room for eating, drinking, and for daytime concealment and night-time sleeping than a smaller creature. A carnivorous hunter will extend his range of movement to match the availability of his prey and his own capabilities. Small monkeys do not usually roam beyond a half-mile radius of the forest feeding-grounds; baboons in troops of forty can range over some forty miles; gorillas in much smaller groups normally keep within ten miles of their home base. The early Nimrods, however, would eventually traverse hunting territories as great as those of wolves and wild dogs, who move in packs of ten over hundreds of square miles.

Such expeditions would require of the hominid

participant a high degree of collaborative effort, foresight, courage and singlemindedness of purpose, as well as physical agility and stamina. He needed to be able to make fire to defend himself at night and keep warm, as well as the ability to make stone tools for skinning his prey and weapons to bring them down. Above all, hunting on this scale demands the ability to think logically and to communicate with his fellows, and both activities require speech. *Homo erectus* 360,000 years ago had fire and he had almost certainly developed the very considerable anatomical prerequisites of speech, made initially possible by the erect stance that opened the valve of his pharynx. The fact that he was now a 'mighty Nimrod' and had the elements of a social organisation is evidence that he had also achieved the fine neural and muscle co-ordination necessary for articulate speech. Perhaps this facility above all won him eventual domination over his greatest hominid rival, *Australopithecus*.

Their journeys farther and farther afield in search of game presented Man's hunting ancestors with fresh challenges and enriched their store of experiences. The inadequate, or plain unlucky ones, perished in the open country; the successful returned to their mates to breed offspring more likely to prove themselves 'mighty men' when their turn came to leave home.

However, longer missions in the field necessitated social and biological adjustments, which in turn gave rise to psychological stresses that would endure into modern Man. Already certain physical differences between the sexes had been accentuated. The male frame was better adapted to make the best possible use of his new-found ability to run on two legs, and the wider-hipped female could not keep up with him in the hunting-field. She was left behind to bear and care for her offspring, now no longer able to cling to her on the move. In any case, the extra-uterine development required by the young hominid demanded the mother's full-time attention in more settled conditions than a hunting expedition would permit. A monkey's infant is helpless for only the first year or so of its life, the young of the ape for two or three years, but it has been estimated that the *Homo erectus* baby of half a million years ago would have needed four or five years to attain a degree of self-sufficiency that would enable it to fend for itself.

During that time the hominid mothers would be left by their mates for increasing periods, as the hunters undertook ever more adventurous expeditions away from home. They were thus deprived of male company at the very time when practical assistance and protection would be needed most. If sexual activity had by now assumed a non-oestral continuity, and the family unit had become established as the accepted social grouping of the species, the absence of the male partner would have been more deeply felt than a mere wish for sensual gratification in coitus. Eroticism, as we have seen, was already taking on its wider, social significance; sexual relationships were beginning to demand those qualities of constant comradeship and mutual comfort that we associate with human love.

For the males, long periods away from their mates may have encouraged homosexual activity, the more sensually acceptable now that automatic hormonal control of sexual behaviour had given way to a free selection of partners. If so, this biologically sterile deviation may well have contributed to the increasing sexual dimorphism of the species: the female's need to recapture the attentions of her returned consort from his male companions would have tended to favour those females exhibiting more pronounced secondary sex characteristics to compensate for the diminishing effect of periodic oestral signals.

Sexual dimorphism varies considerably within the animal world: some birds, for instance, are clearly distinguishable as male or female by the colour of their feathers, while others, like the robin, none but the experienced ornithologist can easily tell apart. Among the primates, the male gorilla may be twice as large as any member of his harem, while the only visible difference to be seen in the female gibbon in the wild is the protrusion of nipples through the fur when she has borne young. Among the hominids this matter of overt 'sexiness' became a matter of crucial importance if the species were to survive, and the female responded by developing as permanent features of her physical appearance certain areas of swelling, sensitivity, and colouration normally associated only with periods of sexual anticipation. Her mammary glands expanded far beyond any functional necessity, perhaps, as has been suggested, to mimic those other large, globular appendages, her buttocks, developed before she changed her coital presentation from back to front. The swelling and reddening of her 'lower lips', the vulva, during intercourse became the permanent aspect of the everted and pigmented margins of her mouth. The primate female's oestral flushing signals, hitherto confined to the genital areas, extended to other regions of the body as sexual display signals not confined to periods of 'heat', and now more permanently in view with the loss of body hair. Where hair was retained, in the armpits and around the genitals, it served to distribute the odour-producing substances secreted by the apocrine glands, with which the female of our species is far more richly endowed than the male to advertise her sexual receptivity. In short, the exasperation of the modern 'golf-widow' has a long history in primate development; her recourse to beauty parlour and plastic surgeon was foreshadowed in her hominid predecessor's anatomical adaptations to enable her to compete more effectively in the mating-game.

But too much sexiness can be a bad thing; continual receptiveness in the female is an open invitation to promiscuity, which is a threat to parental pair-bonding.

It must also aggravate the sense of deprivation among less-favoured suitors. Neighbouring young bloods have, as it were, to restrain their ardour and be content to stand and wolf-whistle on the sidewalks. The reader hardly needs reminding that the stresses in society which this new situation engendered among our hominid ancestors persisted into the next evolutionary grade of *Homo sapiens*. Man has found it necessary to adopt a number of measures designed to dampen down our instinctive responses to sexual display signals. Among the most primitive people living in the hottest climates it is often customary to wear some garment to cover the genitalia and other powerfully evocative display regions of the body, or to adopt some cultural means of physically separating the sexes until they are in a position to establish a permanent pair-bonding relationship and bring up children. Similarly, nature has herself provided a hymenal 'seal' in the virgin's vagina for making the initial coitus that much more difficult for the young, inexperienced female to conceive an offspring before she or her partner is ready to provide it with the security necessary for its survival.

Such natural and artificial restrictions to free sexual indulgence have their price. A perpetual state of tension arises between the natural inclinations of the sexually-alert adolescent and the demands of family and communal life. From being a simple reflex action for reproductive copulation, triggered by certain visual and olfactory stimuli, sex has become an end in itself, involving a wide range of emotions, many of them in continual conflict. The sex-urge in Man has therefore a wider and more emotive significance than obtains in the lower animals, and commands more of our attention than its biological importance would seem to warrant. After all, we do not contemplate our more vital functions of sleeping and breathing with the same apprehension and diffidence that we feel about sex; we have not thought it necessary to send out plain-clothes policemen snooping around seamy bookshops and flea-pit cinemas in our cities for evidence that pornographers have been exhibiting pictures of human beings publicly shovelling food into their mouths.

Sexual frustration and deviation are the unhappy by-products of Man's evolutionary and technical progress. While such emotional instability can give impetus to creative thought, as we have remarked earlier, it produces an area of discontent which family intimacy and mutual reassurance can only partly assuage and must in many respects only exacerbate. The Oedipal stresses that modern Man has inherited are just one product of conflicting sexual interests within the family. When parental ties are broken by the needs of a hunting economy, the lonely mother must seek elsewhere for her comfort. It has been suggested that the incest taboos that are almost universal in human societies stem from this stage in our evolution. Certainly, the avoidance of sexual relations between parents and their children, or between sibs, is not instinctive, in the sense that the male baboon will instinctively spurn a female not in heat. It is rather a cultural inhibition derived from the kind of situation prevalent in any hunting community when the patriarchal male is absent for long periods from the family. But the taboo is so deep-seated and ubiquitous that one is tempted to believe that its transmission is genetic, that is, that the guilt and abhorrence that incestuous behaviour arouses in most humans must be somehow programmed into our genes.

Eventually such sexual customs and inhibitions acquired a religious authority, and their observance was laid upon the pious conscience of the believer. But the motivations for such deep-seated, and probably pre-human taboos must have long preceded the concept of a tribal god as the custodian of his people's sexual discipline; and their ultimate sanction was less concerned with fear of divine retribution, like that which overtook the libidinous city of Sodom in the book of

Genesis, than with the disruption to be expected in a hunting community when social rivalries threaten its cohesion. One is reminded of the care exercised by such mighty Nimrods as the American Indians to regulate marital alliances between clans on the basis of supposed pre-human, totemic ancestors (see Chapter Nine).

5

A Mind Divided

That unease of conscience that Man developed as a means of exercising control over his primary instincts is a unique characteristic of *Homo sapiens*. The separation of the mind into its subconscious and conscious levels which is implicit in the supervisory process makes logical reasoning possible. While the one level freely indulges itself in receiving and recording instantaneous impressions from the senses, the other tries to sift and marshal the information they convey into the straight lines of conceptual thought. It is at this level that we organise our daily lives, it is from that rich storehouse of past experience, individually perceived or, as some would maintain, genetically inherited, that the religious visionary obtains his glimpses of 'reality'; it is his window onto heaven. By dulling the critical faculties of his consciousness through some sort of self-hypnosis, the mystic pulls aside the curtains of the subconscious and allows himself to be dazzled and overwhelmed by the intensity of images projected from the past.

The prophet shares his ability to dissociate mentally with the creative artist and the schizophrenic. Genius, as we know, often borders on madness, and society has shown itself willing to extend an unusual tolerance to such gifted individuals in recognition of the benefits their visions and voices might bring to the 'sane' world. The manner and degree of their ecstasy ('standing outside oneself') varies greatly according to local cultural traditions, but all share the underlying belief that it is possible to penetrate the limits of human awareness by spontaneous intuition, and thus bypass the normal reasoning processes. However sceptically we may treat such 'instant' revelations, recognising them for the most part as being no more than the disordered impressions of past experience, the prophet finds many ready to accept his claims to special knowledge and to believe that he has indeed seen the face of God and heard His Word. His 'revelation' finds a response in the hearts of his followers because he is drawing ultimately upon that reservoir of human experience that is common to us all. And because the believer can find here the comfort and reassurance of a shared understanding, he will be inspired with renewed confidence in himself and his mission in life, and find peace of mind amid all its uncertainties.

The price demanded for the intellectual and spiritual benefits of Man's divided mind is the frustration of conflicting desires. Popular psychology has acquainted us all with the dangers of frustration through the suppression of our natural inclinations, and it may be that an obsession with these fears has led to the excesses of self-indulgence characteristic of some aspects of our 'permissive' society. But some frustration of our impulses can be intellectually rewarding if the damming of the libido in one direction leads to the application of a compensatory effort elsewhere. Examples abound in the arts and sciences where the attainment of exceptional skills has been bought at the cost of satisfactory sexual or family relationships.

It seems, therefore, that in every field of human intellectual endeavour, in the arts, sciences, and in religion, the divided mind bequeathed to us by our evolutionary heritage has been the greatest single factor in our success as a species. Whether we shall survive to enjoy our triumph for very long depends largely on our ability to resolve this inherited discontent by other means than self-destruction. For while it is one thing for the creative artist and scientist to sacrifice his peace of mind for the sake of his genius, the emotional stress for most of us cannot be directed outwards to great works. It tends to build up within us, threatening our equanimity and the harmony of our social and family relationships.

Some would maintain that religious faith provides that necessary relief for our inbuilt anxieties, and define this aspect of religion as a system of shared experiences, emotional, physical, and intellectual, directed to just that end. Certainly today the religious phenomenon is so universal among men that we must assume that this inclination to dissociate periodically from more rational thought and constructive action is a kind of release-valve designed to relieve the stresses imposed upon us by the divided mind. In that case, we might expect to find some such 'displacement activity' already indulged in by those lower primates whose life-style might otherwise lead us to think that they are similarly subject to the emotional strains of conflicting urges.

Something of the kind may be the explanation for a remarkable ritual dance performed by chimpanzees in the rain-forests of Tanzania, observed by Jane Goodall:

> At about noon the first heavy drops of rain began to fall. The chimpanzees climbed out of the tree and, one after the other, plodded up the steep grassy slope towards the open ridge at the top. There were seven adult males in the group, including Goliath and David Greybeard, several females, and a few youngsters. As they reached the ridge the chimpanzees paused. At that moment the storm broke. The rain was torrential and the sudden clap of thunder, right overhead, made me jump. As if this was a signal, one of the big males stood upright and, as he swayed and staggered rhythmically from foot to foot, I could just hear the rising crescendo of his pant-hoots above the beating of the rain. Then he charged off, flat-out down the slope towards the trees he had just left. He ran some thirty yards and then, swinging round the trunk of a small tree to break his head-long rush, leapt into the low branches and sat motionless.
>
> Almost at once two other males charged after him. One of them broke off a branch from a tree as he ran and brandished it in the air before hurling it ahead of him. The other, as he reached the end of his run, stood upright and rhythmically swayed the branches of a tree back and forth, before seizing a huge bough and dragging it farther down the slope. A fourth male, as he too charged, leapt into a tree and, almost without

breaking his speed, tore off a large branch, leapt with it to the ground and continued down the slope. As the last two males called and charged down, so the one who had started the whole performance climbed from his tree and began plodding up the slope again. The others, who had also climbed into the trees near the bottom of the slope, followed suit. And then, when they reached the ridge, they started charging down all over again, one after the other, with equal vigour.

The females and youngsters had climbed into trees near the top of the rise as soon as the displays had begun, and there they remained watching throughout the whole performance. As the males charged down and plodded back up, so the rain fell harder and harder, jagged forks or brilliant flares of lightning lit the leaden sky and the crashing of the thunder seemed to shake the very mountains.

My enthusiasm was not merely scientific as I watched, enthralled.... I could only watch, and marvel at the magnificence of those splendid creatures. With a display of strength and vigour such as this, primitive man himself might have challenged the elements.

Twenty minutes from the start of the performance the last of the males plodded back up the slope for the last time. The females and youngsters climbed down from their trees and the whole group moved over the crest of the ridge. One male paused and, with his hand on a tree-trunk, looked back – the actor taking his final curtain. Then he too vanished over the ridge.

I continued to sit for a while, staring almost in disbelief at the white scars on the tree-trunks and the discarded branches on the grass – all that remained, in that rain-lashed landscape, to prove that the wild 'rain dance' had taken place at all. (*In the Shadow of Man*, p. 62f.)

Clearly the violence of the storm had evoked this defiant response from the animals; the alternative would have been to huddle paralysed with fear beneath some rude shelter and allow their natural anxieties to have the upper hand. Rather than submit to the humiliation of acknowledging the superior power of the elements, the chimps sought refuge in a pattern of behaviour, clearly long established and ritualistic, which restored their self-respect. Performers and onlookers shared in the reassuring experience and together achieved their object of mental equanimity. Had the animals been human beings, we might have been tempted to assume that the intention of the dance was to avert the rainstorm, or to appease the god of thunder; but the purpose here was clearly subjective, to seek relief for their own immediate distress.

In a human situation, some similar tension-relieving 'displacement activity' has been noted among the Samburu tribe of Northern Kenya. In this case it is a natural response to the build-up of stress in virile young men sexually repressed. The younger warriors of the tribe, called *morans,* are obliged from the years of fifteen to thirty to live as bachelors, and remain thus in a state of prolonged adolescence. They find relief for their frustration in periodic lapses into a state of trance, marked by uncontrollable body-shaking. Typical trigger-situations include the out-dancing of one group of *morans* by rivals, humiliating them before their women, or when one of their women is led away in marriage, or when the *morans* are undergoing the rigours of initiation ceremonies, or when they are being replaced by a new age-group of younger men. These shaking-fits may occur on parade, or when a party is ambushed in the field. The trances are not regarded as shameful or deserving of rebuke, but are considered quite normal by the rest of the tribe. When the *morans* are eventually received into adult status and marry, the shaking-bouts cease and would thereafter be considered inappropriate to their new situation.

Similarly, among the Abelam tribe of New Guinea, young deprived bachelors sometimes dissociate mentally and run amok in bursts of uncontrolled violence, making hysterically agitated gestures. This disruptive behaviour is also tolerated by the community and, indeed, earns for the young men some measure of respect.

Such human religious rituals and symbolism share a common function in relieving stress, but their overt actions and invocations may be directed to fulfilling quite dissimilar subsidiary purposes like rain-making, inducing crop and animal fertility, success in battle, and so on. We tend to regard these secondary motivations as primary and categorise religions anthropologically on that basis as nature religions, fertility cults, or veneration of the martial arts. But if we are to understand what makes human beings religious we should look deeper into the evolutionary origin of those psychological stresses that make us seek reassurance in some power outside ourselves. At least to the stage of *Homo erectus* we can find here common ground; thereafter it is possible that the various hominid subspecies went their separate ways geographically and crossed the *sapiens* threshold independently at different times. It would be reasonable then to expect 'knowing Man' to express his religious impulses in a variety of ways to suit his racial characteristics and local environment.

Again the precise means of obtaining emotional relief must depend upon the depth of ecstatic trance demanded by individual needs and tribal custom. The formal worship of Anglican Christianity in an Anglo-Saxon community, for instance, operates usually within very restrained and conventional limits compared with the less inhibited Afro-American Bible sects of the Deep South; even the impassioned oratory of a Methodist revival-meeting in England would seem to the average church-goer a breach of good taste and an unwarranted display of emotional extravagance. More primitive peoples in their religious festivals deliberately set out to disorientate their minds by such methods of mass hypnosis as dancing to the point of exhaustion, monotonous repetition of words and phrases, rhythmic drumming or stamping, uncontrolled jerking, twirling, or head shaking, thereby inducing in themselves and their companions a 'hypnoid', or trance state, in which the conscious mind is opened up to the 'inspiration' or suggestion of its subconscious levels. At the same time, free rein is also given to suppressed emotions in a socially acceptable way, thus forestalling more dangerous explosions.

The psychological mechanism of the religious trance is well enough known; in fact, it is essentially the same as that employed by the shock-therapist treating a neurotic patient. He will try, through hypnosis, drugs, or electrical shock-treatment, to produce a crisis-state in his subject's nervous system that will arouse him to 'abreact', that is, to rehearse in his conscious mind the traumatic events that brought about his hysterical condition. For example, a victim of shell-shock can be made to re-live the nightmare of the trenches that so disturbed his mind, and which thereafter he has tried to blot from his memory. By forcing it to the light of consciousness under controlled conditions, the patient can be persuaded to go once more through that dreadful experience, step by step, horror by horror, until at last, goaded to breaking point by the psychiatrist's remorseless probing, his nervous system breaks down and the subject suffers a complete emotional collapse. When he returns to normal, he will often express his relief in floods of tears, or in shaking his head and smiling, and pronounce himself wonderfully free of that burden of anxiety that had beset him. From then on he will be able to recall the events at will, so that the awful memory is not left to fester in his subconscious, exerting its baneful influence on the balance of his mind.

This treatment has produced remarkable results among victims of battle neuroses in two world wars, but the principle involved has a much wider reference for the human condition. Through such climactic orgasms of excitement, stimulated by fear, anger, or sexual passion, it is possible to relieve stresses and strains that are more persistent and deep-seated than those generated by a single traumatic shock. The psychiatrists found that it was not always necessary to stir the excitement of the neurotic patient by concentrating his attention upon the particular situation that caused the initial trauma; any fear-provoking stimuli could be used to create the necessary crisis and thus clear the brain of its accumulated tension. So, over a much wider field of human experience, the strains that must inevitably develop in the divided mind of *Homo sapiens* can be relieved periodically by similar emotional crises aroused in a variety of ways.

Religious sentiment embraces many kinds of emotion, including fear, sorrow, joy, lust, hatred, all of which may be carried to extremes. In the less inhibited cults, the intensity of excitement generated during worship can drive the devotee into a trance or 'possession'. In this highly suggestible state, some areas of the brain become sensitised and receptive, while others may suffer strong inhibition, amounting even to paralysis. Thus, on the one hand, the subject may feel himself divinely inspired and credit every random impression received from without, or projected from his own subconscious, as a 'revelation' of eternal truth, and, on the other hand, become inured to a level of pain that would otherwise be well beyond his normal threshold of tolerance. In every case, the usual processes of the mind are disturbed, critical faculties suspended, and the believer is suddenly freed from the burden of his own individuality. He can resign himself to being 'taken over' by the god or controlling spirit, and achieves thereby a wonderful sense of inner peace.

It is this psychiatry that motivates the revivalist meeting and the political convention. The hell-fire speaker and the ranting demagogue can so stir audiences into a state of extreme emotion that the more susceptible souls present will pass into a hypnoid condition, where they are easily persuaded into adopting beliefs and attitudes they would otherwise reject or ignore. Such 'conversions' may not be so sudden as they seem, for the stresses and anxieties that brought their subjects to the mission or convention may have been building up for some time previously; it needed but the mounting excitement and the hypnotic effect of the speaker's words uttered in an atmosphere of tense expectancy to trigger the release mechanism. The wave of emotion breaks, and the 'convert' responds unreservedly to the call of the Master. His doubts and personal misgivings are swept aside, for now he is a child of God (or the State), his sins (or deviationisms) are forgiven, and he knows the 'peace which passeth all understanding'. This sense of well-being may not last long; it is likely that a new set of inhibitions will gather around him, encouraging fresh doubts and building up another head of emotional steam that will need some further climactic release.

The increased suggestibility of a hypnoid subject is a factor that the practising psychoanalyst watches carefully. It is too easy for a patient repeatedly treated in this way to suffer what the Freudians call a 'transference situation', in which, in his state of extreme sensitivity, he fastens upon every word uttered by the psychiatrist as inspired, and every wish or suggestion as a divine command. The evangelist and the politician may welcome this attachment, supremely confident that their way and teaching is the best, and that they are themselves the servants of Truth. The wise psychiatrist knows better and tries to divert his patient's devotion into more discerning and critical attitudes.

The true shaman, or inspired priest, invites his audience to identify themselves with him in his séance, but only that they may thereby share his communion with the elemental powers in the universe. The word *shaman* is a Siberian term used particularly among the Tungus reindeer herders to denote a religious leader who, in an ecstatic trance, ascends to heaven on 'trips'. He can also penetrate to the realms of the dead, and sometimes he will describe his long journey in a chant. His actions and costume symbolise the inner meaning of the ceremonies in which he takes part. His garb is usually indicative of the animal spirits who act as his guides in the other world, and he therefore dresses himself in their skins or feathers, and will imitate their voices. Sometimes he symbolises his ascent into heaven by climbing a tree or a ladder, or he will claim that he is riding to heaven on the back of a goose.

The questions he tries to answer will concern some matter of particular communal importance, like a famine or epidemic. On the other hand, he may be trying to heal a sick person, and in this case he must pursue the soul of the afflicted suppliant down into the underworld, and there overcome with his superior powers the hostile spirits who are trying to prevent the patient's soul from returning to his body. The shaman may also act as a soothsayer and respond to individual questions submitted to him by anxious enquirers in his audience.

Professor Shirokogoroff, the eminent Russian authority on the Tungus, describes a shamanistic séance in this way:

> The rhythmic music and singing, and later the dancing of the shaman, gradually involve every participant more and more in collective action. When the audience begins to repeat the refrains together with the assistants, only those who are defective fail to join in the chorus. The tempo of the action increases; the shaman with a spirit is no more an ordinary man or relative, but is a 'placing' (i.e. incarnation) of the spirit; the spirit acts together with the audience, and this is felt by everyone. The state of many participants is now near to that of the shaman himself, and only a strong belief that when the shaman is there the spirit may only enter him, restrains the participants from being possessed in mass by the spirit. This is a very important condition of shamanising which does not however reduce mass susceptibility to the suggestion, hallucinations, and unconscious acts produced in a state of mass ecstasy. When the shaman feels that the audience is with him and follows him, he becomes still more active and this effect is transmitted to his audience. After shamanising, the audience recollects various moments of the performance, their great pyscho-physiological emotion and the hallucinations of sight and hearing which they have experienced. They then have a deep satisfaction – much greater than that from emotions produced by theatrical and musical performances, literature and general artistic phenomena of the European complex, because in shamanising the audience at the same times acts and participates. (*Psychomental Complex of the Tungus*, London, 1935; quoted by I. M. Lewis, *Ecstatic Religion*, Harmondsworth, 191, p. 53.)

In a more secular context, much the same hysteria occurs among teenage girls at pop festivals, under the inspiration of their guitar-twanging, pubes-thrusting 'shamans' on the stage. The main difference between these and more serious release-rituals is that there the control of the participants, their initial stimulation, their urging to a climax, and, most important, their gradual run-down to normality, is firmly in the hands of the dance-leader and his acolytes; we have to call in the police and St John Ambulance Brigade.

But, after all, true religious release-rituals are not games and weekend frolics; they are necessary devices by which communities try to relieve the bio-psychological tensions in a way that offers the individual support and the social group a vehicle for joint action. The object of adoration is of less moment, provided he, she, or it can serve as an acceptable focus for the congregation's emotions and invite some measure of self-identification. The wise shaman, like the practising psychiatrist, will avoid the kind of personal transference openly courted by the politician and the pop-singer through their publicity agents.

The essential feature of all effective release-rituals should be one of emotional relief and inner contentment, with the participant left feeling guilt-free and relaxed. If it is otherwise, some vital element is missing or, as is particularly common in over-rationalised faiths, some unacceptably precise formulation of theological concepts has hindered the complete absorption of the conscious mind, and demanded of the intelligent worshipper an intolerable sacrifice of his intellectual integrity. The resultant anxiety then merely adds to the burden of guilt, since the harassed religionist seems to be faced with a choice between honesty and piety. Such 'rational religions' were desperately sought among intellectual Christians of the nineteenth century, to counter the influence of those new schools of biblical criticism whose intent seemed to be only the discrediting of traditional interpretations, by exposing the inconsistencies of Holy Writ. But no philosophy or dogmatic theology can adequately fulfil the function of religious absolution, however intellectually satisfying. The Greeks, with their flair for compromise, managed to combine mysticism with a healthy, rational scepticism. Their mockery of the traditional gods and goddesses indulging in amorous buffoonery in the Olympian bed-chambers did not prevent intelligent Greeks from acknowledging the need of ordinary mortals for some emotional release from the pressures of day-to-day living. They made their mythologies the stage on which to enact religious dramas that offered them relief from their frustrations, and they threw themselves into the emotional embrace of their mystery cults. They did not fall into the error of their more pedantic cultural successors who demand that biblical myths be historical fact, and prophetic oracles some kind of Old Moore's Almanack.

Our own tormented Christian civilisation is seeking some similar solution, either by rejecting the Church's dogmatism in favour of the esoteric teaching of the East, or, more sadly, by piously reverting to the uncritical days of 'fundamentalist' Christianity, and the call of the Bible-thumping salvationist.

In summary, then, the stresses imposed upon *Homo sapiens* by the need to control his instinctive drives in the interests of social and domestic harmony can find some relief in mental dissociation. In religious terms, this has given the mystic and the shaman a means of access to a rich store of subconscious impressions whose immediacy and vividness have claimed for them a divine origin and authority. For lesser mortals, the transports of religious ecstasy in church or village square have offered a controlled and socially acceptable outlet for suppressed emotions. The problem that has grown with Man's increasing self-constraint is that to avail himself of this psychological therapy he must relax that very faculty for rational motivation that has brought him where he is; the cause of his distress is the chief obstacle to its relief.

6

Submission

We saw in Chapter Three that the social organisation of most primates requires the establishment of a dominance hierarchy. Normally one animal is in overall control of a unit, and in the case of large groups like baboons, subordinate ranks range below him in a pyramid of generally-accepted 'pecking-orders'. This authoritative arrangement helps to preserve the cohesion of the group and ensures adequate territorial defence, optimum selectivity in breeding, and sometimes collaboration in hunting. Smaller, family-type units, as we meet among gorillas, are more simply structured, but there is normally a dominant male to whom the females and young show due deference when occasion demands.

This need for a dominance system is deeply rooted in animal consciousness. Even when infant apes have been reared in human domestic situations, where they are not at risk physically or socially, they soon demonstrate their inborn need to know where they stand in the dominance pattern of their adoptive society. They will, like human children, test the resistance of their new guardian's authority by rebelliousness and fractious behaviour, what we should call 'sheer naughtiness'. If they meet with unshakable resolve to maintain parental discipline, they will submit and be satisfied, and thereafter, knowing their situation, relax to enjoy the society of those about them. There is no shame in accepting one's inferior position in the primate group's hierarchy; it is the natural order of things that some animals will dominate others, and, although the mantle of leadership may occasionally be snatched by a challenger, the well-being of the group as a whole, and the peace of mind of its individual members, can only be assured if authoritarianism is quickly re-established and generally accepted.

This same need for a dominance system has persisted into the human species where it forms the basis of our family and political relationships. We, all of us, at some stage in our lives, need to be dominated. We organise our societies into hierarchies. We may pay lip-service to democracy, and dream of the day when we shall all be free, and sometimes, indeed, we slaughter one another in order to achieve this liberation; but at heart we are more inclined to 'baboonism' than the easy-going paternalism of the gorilla. We like to have our behavioural guidelines drawn for us; like the young child pushing for the first time against authority, it is good to know what the limits are. Even our most vicious and depraved delinquents usually have their gang-leaders and gang-rules to be obeyed without question.

So we appoint our kings, priests, judges, and warlords, dress them in tall hats, seat them on raised thrones, and expect them to address us in an antiquated and barely comprehensible language; in short, we enhance their stature and dignity by making them as different from us, their subjects, as possible. And over them all we place our gods.

To be at all worthy of their status and function, our deities must be all-powerful; they must dominate us. However we conceive of our own tribal god, as superman, super-animal, or super-force, he, she, or it must have the capabilities of influencing our thoughts and determining our future, penalising rebelliousness and rewarding obedience to the divine will. If we fail to conform, we 'sin', and the resulting breakdown in communications can be restored only by some atoning sacrifice on our part, and an attitude of submission in penitence. Even if, as mortals, we cannot understand the divine plan, it is an article of religious faith that it nevertheless exists and gives our lives their purpose. So long as we can remain convinced of the god's reality and the validity of his grand design for us as individuals, we can meet the slings and arrows of outrageous fortune with equanimity. Real submission then brings peace to our anxious minds, for it removes our fears for the unknowable future.

It was not until *Homo sapiens* had developed his faculty for reasoning ahead and, through his wonderful gift of imagination, could begin to terrorise himself with visions of impending doom, that this need for a super-dominant baboon would have been felt. The mortal boss of a pack or tribe could fail in his effectiveness as protector or progenitor. The façade of superiority would crack, and with it, his authority and the cohesiveness of the group. Man's peace of mind needed a divine leader who would brook no opposition, whose authority was paramount and unchallengeable; whose rules once ordained were immutable and eternal. Such a dominant superior could alone command Man's respect and give him the reassurance for the future his restless imagination longed for. Then, so long as he obeyed the god's rules, however bizarre or even painful they may appear by rational standards, he could feel secure. The crops might fail, his animals or children die, or he himself pass through the valley of the shadow of death, but the comforting self-assurance that he had done his best to keep within the set limits, and had atoned for his transgressions with the required sacrifices in their due time, would sustain him.

The religious ordinances that are willingly accepted by believers for the sake of their piety make enquirers from other cultures sometimes gape in astonishment. We see young children in primitive societies being forced by their parents to undergo the most painful and violent assaults upon their bodies and minds in the name of their tribal god (see Chapter Seven), and in every age men and women have cheerfully mutilated their flesh and personalities to conform to 'divine' precepts. Even in our supposedly advanced culture, we tolerate extraordinary interference with the most intimate aspects of our sexual lives, accepting instruction from our priests on when and how to copulate and breed children, and even applaud young devotees when they renounce the joys of married life entirely for the sake of religious celibacy.

On the other hand, religion has given the peoples of the world a kind of supra-tribal morality which, however limited and perhaps in the long run harmful to our survival as a species, has imposed over large sections of mankind some broad principles of conduct, and set guidelines which give us a certain feeling of security. Man's concern for the sanctity of life and the maintenance of a balance in nature is largely instinctive and commands a wide measure of universal assent (see Chapter Nine). Such concepts have formed the basis of human taboos and natural inhibitions the world over and have been incorporated into otherwise widely differing religious cultures. Those deists who maintain the unity of divine revelation have found no difficulty in discovering among the diverse religions of mankind common elements concerned with the rights of the individual, the integrity of the family, respect for the aged, belief in an after-life, and so on, which have seemed to them certain evidence for the existence of one God disseminating His will among men.

The danger of codifying such precepts of 'natural justice' into bodies of divinely-instituted law is that they thereafter become immutable and self-perpetuating; they cannot be changed or superseded without destroying the authority of our super-baboons and disrupting the sense of security which was the underlying purpose of their creation. While Man's cultural and technological progress proceeded slowly, from hunting and gathering to the dawn of agriculture and urbanisation, extending over hundreds of thousands of years, those basic concepts were valid and proved their worth in ensuring the survival of the species and the establishment of harmonious relationships between widely scattered communities of *Homo sapiens*. But the last ten thousand years have seen a rapid advance in the technologies of food-production and travel, and in the last few hundred years particularly, of harnessing natural resources for power and organising resistance to disease, all of which combine to threaten our continued existence on an overcrowded planet. Man has begun to influence his own evolutionary development, and to infringe those taboos that have hitherto formed the basis of his gods' commandments. Biological life can be preserved almost indefinitely, and can no longer be considered 'sacred' on its own account; increasingly someone has to decide when to pull the plug, stop the drugs, or let the fever take its course, when the moral value of such artificially prolonged life is deemed of less worth than the cost of its preservation. Our new technologies are producing different kinds of human society that demand fresh standards and differently drawn boundaries of acceptable behaviour. We are having to choose between a gradual breakdown in the traditional bastions of authority as their inadequacy becomes increasingly obvious, or a short, sharp confrontation with our old gods and their replacement by fresh 'super-baboons'. In either case, human society is bound to be disrupted, with even chances that Man will destroy himself before he has found and accepted a new dominant hierarchy.

The philosopher's dream, that Man may one day be able to break out of the old dominance system and rule his own life rationally within a kind of easy-going, gibbon-gorilla family structure, voluntarily co-operating with his fellows for the good of all, comes up against the hard fact that human nature has inherited a social attitude more characteristic of baboons than of our nearer primate relations. We still want to be dominated and are happy to accept standards passed onto us by generations of dominated baboons. We believe the unlikely or downright impossible because we prefer not to challenge our traditions. We accept uncritically highly debatable religious tenets because they provide us with a framework of understanding within which life has some grand, overall purpose. Without it our existence would seem to lack meaning, and it is inconceivable that we should have been created by our super-baboon to no higher end than that sufficing lesser forms of life, the maintenance of a divine spark on an otherwise dead planet.

Even our gestures of submission to the deity are no less primitive. The worshipper's deep obeisance, kneeling, genuflexion, casting down of eyes, kissing of hands, and so on, are all related to the primate submission displays. Before a dominant animal, a gorilla will often try to avert aggression by lowering its head and cowering down, with arms and legs tucked under its body as if to protect them from attack. A human captive adopts just such an attitude when begging for mercy, and among the Nyakyusa people of Tanganyika it is the customary posture of a woman greeting a man. To the Hindus this is the most reverential form of salutation. It is called *sashtanga*, 'with-eight-limbs', because eight parts of the body touch the ground in token of complete submission, two hands, two feet, two knees, forehead, and breast. It is used by a pupil before his guru, or a subject before his king. It is a sign of deep contrition, as when a man seeks readmission into his caste after he has been excommunicated (B. Walker, *The Hindu World*, ii, 1968, p. 342).

When a female chimpanzee crouches submissively in this way before a male, the gesture has a rather different origin. She turns away from a potential aggressor and displays her rump towards him, inviting sexual intercourse. Even though she may not be in heat, the male will mount her and make a token thrust or two to demonstrate his superiority, without intending or even necessarily desiring proper copulation.

The Nyakyusa woman mentioned above, in addition

to crouching in humble obeisance before a man from her tribe, must also turn her head away to avoid looking directly at him. This, too, is a submissive gesture of primate origin, for we see it demonstrated among apes as a counteractive response to the common threat-signal of staring hard at one's opponent beneath frowning brows. We still feel it necessary to warn our children against staring at people: 'It's rude.' So, before our superiors and our gods we incline our heads and avert our eyes as a sign of humility.

When we bow lower and remove our headgear out of respect, we are making a submissive gesture with yet another connotation. As a general rule, a dominant animal must appear physically larger than his opponent. A common threat or courtship display is to make some part of the body or its covering swell up or bristle, and many creatures are equipped by nature with air-sacs as part of their respiratory systems, to blow them up like balloons, or with special patches of fur or feathers that they can expand or erect at will, to give the appearance of greater size. The corresponding submission signals will therefore have the general effect of diminishing stature, by settling fur back sleekly on the body, letting the tail droop between the legs, laying cocked ears flat against the head, and, in our case, by kneeling, curtsying, or removing our hats in the presence of our superiors, mortal or divine. To emphasise our own inferiority even further, we provide the objects of our worship and homage with halos, cocked hats, crowns, crested or spiked helmets, and the like, and set them high above the crowd on pillars and platforms.

The gesture of imparted grace and authority, known as 'laying on of hands', is well known in the ecclesiastical ritual of the Church. Outside this ceremonial context, patting the head or shoulder is, of course, a common enough indication of reassurance by a superior to an inferior in any culture, be it no more than a sign of parental approval and affection. But it has a long primate history. Between chimpanzees this gesture on greeting implies that no aggression is intended, and the junior animal thus touched is calmed and reassured when meeting with a more senior companion. One chimp will reach out and touch the other's body with the flat of his hand, or with the back of slightly flexed fingers. The touch may be directed towards his head, or to his shoulder or back, but, significantly, the hand is often placed upon the other's groin, thigh, or directly upon the genitals. One is reminded of the submissive gesture made by Joseph in the Old Testament story, when he laid his hand upon his dying father's groin (Genesis 47: 29).

There are other indications that such greeting/submission signals have a sexual origin. A female chimpanzee in heat will normally be touched in greeting upon her sexual swelling, without the gesture necessarily implying a wish to copulate. Again, when two males move towards each other, uttering their characteristic soft, panting grunts of recognition, or when they run together and more demonstratively fling their arms about each other, their excitement is often accompanied by pronounced penile erections (Goodall, *Primate Behaviour*, ed. I. DeVore, New York, 1965, p. 471). The idea seems to be that, by making some form of sexual gesture or display, as if inviting a mating response, the potentially threatened animal is diverting the aggressor from any hostile intent. Sexual activity is incompatible with real hostility, so making the first moves in this direction inhibits less friendly actions. Such greeting signals then come under the category of 'displacement actions', that is, behaviour which seems irrelevant and out of context in the situation at hand. Natural selection has acted upon certain of these actions like touching, or patting, by enhancing their effectiveness as communicatory signals. As a result they have become stereotyped, or ritualised, and have been inherited by *Homo sapiens* for use in both religious and secular circumstances (see George B. Schaller, *The Year of the Gorilla,* London, 1965, p. 238f.).

Another manual sign of submission occasionally seen among chimpanzees is that of an attacked animal holding out its hand towards the aggressor, not, in this case, to touch it in greeting, but as a voluntary surrender of a vulnerable part of the body as if to invite attack. In fact, the weaker animal knows well that the stronger will not inflict any really disabling injury upon one of its own species; that kind of barbarism is specific to Man: lower primates have more regard for the survival of their kind. The dominant chimp is content with accepting the mark of surrender as an assurance that further resistance is not contemplated. Similar tokens of submission are common enough in human combat: necks are stretched out to the victor's sword, throats and breasts bared to the dagger's thrust, weapons thrown down or broken to demonstrate the loser's defencelessness and resignation to his opponent's mercy. In religious contexts this same attitude of utter dependence upon divine grace is often equally required of the penitent believer. Before the dominant Being, Man has no defences; he is naked and helpless, and only by acknowledging his inferiority may he hope to avail himself of his god's unmerited grace.

7

Adolescent Initiation

There comes a time in the life of every child when he must prepare to leave his mother's side and enter the hazardous world of the adult. Adolescence is a difficult period for the growing person, physically and emotionally. A large number of simultaneous adaptations need to be made by the body to fit it for a reproductive and self-sustaining role, and at the same time severe emotional stresses are inevitably imposed by the transition from childhood independence to adult responsibilities.

The young chimpanzee in the wild has a somewhat protracted adolescence in which to become accustomed to his new situation. He reaches puberty when he is between seven and eight years old, but at that stage he is still nowhere near fully grown, a mere forty pounds as against the hundred pounds or so of a mature male. Socially, he has yet another six or seven years to go before he will be allowed to break into the lower ranks of adult hierarchy. Until then he must be content with trying to dominate the females about him, while at the same time learning to treat the older males with more respect. Whereas previously he might have earned himself no more than a rebuke or mild cuff from one of his 'uncles' for some piece of playful impudence, now a similar disregard of authority, or unnecessary disturbance, will bring upon him a demonstration of real anger and severe chastisement. He has to learn the hard way that there are boundaries of behaviour beyond which young, as yet untested, members of the community may not go.

The adolescent chimp finds it hard at first to understand the change of attitude he encounters among older animals who had hitherto allowed him to play around them, and who had even encouraged him to flex his young muscles in his childish assaults upon their persons. Suddenly, it seems, they have become large and menacing, and his previous assumptions that his elders would never do him real harm and would always be at hand to defend him from outside attack, or from the results of his own foolishness, are brutally shattered; he feels hurt and emotionally insecure.

The young chimp will initially find in his mother a source of comfort and a strong stabilising influence to help him through this difficult time. Even when he is ten or eleven years old he will continue to show her proper filial respect. For her part, the female will rally to her son's side if he is attacked by an older male, but, of course, if the aggressor is too high-ranking, there is little she can do but stand on the sidelines, barking her disapproval. When, inevitably, she sees her son run off worsted in the encounter, she will often approach his chastiser submissively and try to placate him with her hand-touching, as if to reassure him that her errant offspring meant no real harm or disrespect.

But for all his mother's continuing affection, the adolescent chimp knows well that his dependence on her must end before long, and that he must learn to accept the dominance of his elders and subject himself to their discipline. Just when he is beginning to be aware of his own individuality and personal strength of mind and body, he runs hard up against this seemingly unyielding wall of authoritarianism. After such encounters, he may retreat to a safe distance and scream and shout in his frustration, drum his feet against the buttresses of trees, rush around dragging branches after him, or indulge in other kinds of displacement activity, but he knows that he will have to go back and persevere with trying to establish relationships with the adult male population. For he has much to learn if he is to live harmoniously within the group, or even survive.

The number of truly instinctive reactions in the

primate, that is, purely automatic responses to nervous stimuli, is surprisingly small. Such advanced animals have learnt much of their basic behaviour by imitation. Even a female chimp kept from infancy in isolation from experienced mothers, will be pathetically ignorant of how to handle and feed her own offspring. Similarly, without the benefit of watching others, a male will be ludicrously inept at mating effectively, however much he may be stimulated to do so by the oestral female's visual and olfactory signals. The adolescent chimp, then, must remain with the adult males and learn their ways, whatever this persistence may cost him in hurt pride, frustration, and physical discomfort.

When the strain of the young chimp's in-between existence becomes too great, he may wander off alone to sulk, sometimes for two or three days on end. But eventually sheer boredom and loneliness will draw him back to the outskirts of male adult society to try and win acceptance and be allowed some share in the privileges of his elders.

When he has reached the age of thirteen or so years, the male chimp will be ready to make serious attempts to break into the lower ranks of the adult hierarchy. At first, he will aim no higher than dominating others of his own age, but any success he achieves here will encourage him to tackle lower-ranking mature males. He will seek out those that seem most likely to flinch or run before his charging displays, but, however successful, the excitement of the challenge will itself often be enough to drive him beyond the normal restraints of caution to take on opponents much higher in the social scale.

However much human children may learn from their parents, and however gently they are ushered through adolescence, they have nevertheless to come face-to-face with basically the same problems of growing up as the chimpanzee. They must learn a fresh set of values as they relate to adult opportunities and responsibilities. They must fight for their place in a much larger society than the home, and be prepared to submit to a firmer and more relentless discipline than a child might normally expect from his mother and father. The more primitive the society, the more dramatic and traumatic is this process of initiation. What a well-established community might try to achieve in its young over many years of patient schooling, beginning long before puberty and lasting through upper school, college, and university into full maturity, more primitive societies have to do in days, weeks, or, at the most, in a few years. For the 'in-between' in a marginal economy, where a man must prove himself fit to defend his tribe in battle before he is allowed to assume the responsibility of adding to its numbers, there is less room for gentle persuasion; adolescent reorientation has to be swift and often savage. If the young man survives his ordeals he will have proved his fitness for manhood and adult status; if he does not, his weakness were best revealed at this early stage lest he later on prove a dangerously inadequate link in the chain of communal defences.

Initiation is usually a religious exercise. The all-pervasive influence of religion plays a vital part in the young person's adoption of his new status and responsibilities. He must accept a more profound allegiance to the tribal god so that, whatever may befall his earthly leader through death, disability, or usurpation, his loyalty to his community will remain intact. At the same time, he must preserve the discipline of the tribal dominance system. The initiate has to be made to recognise that the authority of his elders is divinely ordained, so that rebellion is tantamount to sacrilege. Thus 'baboonism' is given religious sanction.

The young initiate is deemed to have entered upon a new, sacred relationship with the tribal god and his fellow-men. Ritually, he must die to his old, family-centred life, and be born again into a new society. He will be taught fresh sets of values, to scorn the ways of women, the tender solicitude of his mother and sisters, and to seek out and challenge the dangers he has been taught from infancy to avoid. He must learn to be reserved, to have secrets he must not tell even his own mother, to accept pain without tears, and to inflict it on others without guilt.

Initiation ceremonies characteristically include separation of the neophyte from his family surroundings; his 'death', 'burial', and 're-birth'; his indoctrination with ancestral tribal lore; and his acquisition of the manly arts of warfare and hunting. Adolescent initiation is usually associated with the rites of circumcision in boys, and sometimes in girls also, where an entirely valueless and highly dangerous operation involves cutting away the membrane surrounding the sensitive clitoris (*clitoridectomy*). Penile circumcision is almost as pointless for most males; its original cultic justification seems to have been some kind of preparative act for marriage, the glans penis being permanently 'unsheathed' for its entry into the vagina. But in the initiation ceremonies it has become merely a suitable crisis-point in the life of the male adolescent, comparable with the onset of menstruation in girls. As with all such major landmarks in a person's life, crossing the threshold into adulthood is accorded special sanctity.

Often the mutilation of the boy's penis is attended by quite needless cruelty, for physical and psychological torture seem to be necessary prerequisites for the subject's mental reorientation. For example, among the Australian aborigines of the Karadjeri tribe, the neophyte is violently thrust into isolation from the bosom of his family as a prelude to the gruelling rites themselves. He is led away into the bush before dawn, blindfolded, and his ears plugged. Then several operators set about their gruesome task with flint knives. They make an incision at the base of the penis and remove the whole of the organ's epidermis. It is a complicated and risky operation and said to be extremely painful. Three years later, the young man has to undergo the further mutilation of sub-incision.

Other ordeals have included amputation of fingers and tooth extraction, as well as less crippling assaults like tattooing and scarification of the flesh, or cicatrising. All have as their apparent purpose the giving to the initiate of a new personality, marked by a change in his personal appearance. Henceforth the young man will be a different person, bound more closely to the god by virtue of his indoctrination into ancestral secrets and his complete rejection of the pre-initiatory, unregenerate way of life.

The psychology of initiatory rituals is fundamentally that of the religious trance: the individuality of the subject is broken down through fear, pain, and physical exhaustion, and he is reduced to a highly suggestible state in which new beliefs and patterns of social behaviour can be imposed upon his receptive mind. Dr William Sargant observed the process among young initiates of the Samburu tribe in Northern Kenya:

> Severe stress is imposed on the new recruit, by subjecting him to arbitrary and frightening authority, by bewildering him, abusing or ill-treating him, and by telling him that his old values and sentiments are childish, and so inducing in him a state of unease and suggestibility in which new values can easily be drummed into him, and he recovers his self-confidence by accepting them. The initial conditioning techniques may have to be reinforced from time to time by further conditioning procedures, and follow-up indoctrination is considered most important in all types of religious and other conversion. (*The Mind Possessed*, London, 1963, p. 115.)

Dr Sargant draws a parallel between such initiation techniques in so-called 'primitive' tribes and similar methods of reorientating young minds to fresh sets of values in our western societies. He cites the example of the crack military regiments who have to transform their raw recruits from critical individuals into numbered soldiers, loyal to the group and uncritically obedient to commands, sensible and otherwise, for years afterwards. Less martial in its outward aspect, but psychologically hardly less ruthless, was the nineteenth-century English public school system, whose traditions still linger on in some of our educational establishments.

The initiation of girls in primitive societies follows the same pattern as that ordained for their adolescent brothers: segregation, breaking down of the old customs and values, and indoctrination into the secret arts of adulthood. Here again, it is primarily a religious exercise, and occurs at a crisis-point in the girl's life, in her case the onset of menstruation. It is, therefore, a more personally determined occasion than a boy's circumcision, and the rites are accordingly more individual.

At the first sign of the menses, the girl is taken from her family and set apart, often in a corner of a hut or other shelter, out of sight of the sun. She must feed herself with uncooked food, and wear some special garment or colour that is exclusively her own. Her period of initiation will vary according to the particular culture, but may be any time from the three days of her menstruation, as in India, to several years, as in Cambodia. But after her initial isolation, she will join with other young adepts and receive indoctrination at the hands of older women into the esoteric traditions of feminine adulthood. These will include the domestic arts like spinning, often associated with magic and thus dangerous, and sexuality. The feminine ritual songs and dances they are taught at this time are usually erotic in character, even obscene.

Popular folklore has always maintained a curiously ambivalent attitude towards menstruation. On the one hand, menstrual blood was regarded as a highly malignant substance, and on the other, prized as the most powerful source of life. Being the prime constituent in the creative process, as it was believed, it was charged with power and thus highly dangerous (see Chapter Twelve). The menstruant, then, and everything connected with her is taboo, unapproachable and contagious. She is ritually 'unclean', and to be avoided at all costs, a fastidiousness which has little to do with questions of hygiene.

Many of the cultural prescriptions for the avoidance of menstruants in society may seem strange and even repugnant to us in the western world, but the taboo that attaches to menstrual blood is almost universal throughout mankind. One is inclined to suspect that, like the similar inhibition against incest (see above, p. 41), avoidance of barren sexual contact with a woman at this stage in her reproductive cycle is somehow genetically contrived, necessitated in the developing primate by the change to non-oestral availability in the female. In due course, this reluctance to mate with a menstruant would then have been given a religious sanction, and added to the numinous aura that surrounds feminine sexuality. The crisis-point which marks the feminine adolescent's initiation in adulthood is thus a kind of sacrament by which she is received into a new relationship with the natural world. From that time on she shares with other women access to the awful mystery of generation, and may approach the throne of the Mother-goddess in whom all life originates and is perpetuated (see Chapter Twelve).

To summarise: the transition in every child's life from infancy to responsible adulthood is clearly represented among the primates. Not surprisingly, that fundamental change in human society has been expressed in religious terms and serves to bind the young initiate more firmly into his community and to strengthen his allegiance to the tribal god. By various physical and psychological means the adolescent is prised apart from his old family loyalties and affections and forced to submit to the authority of the clan, often apotheosised in the person of the deity. The mythology of initiation includes the concept of rebirth, while the ritual dramatises the initiate's adoption of a new personality to suit his changed status in society. The female adolescent's entry into adulthood is often associated with her first menstruation, after which she may be introduced into the mysteries of her femininity and the powers that she will thereafter exercise in her role of potential mother, protégée of the divine Creatress of all life.

8

Life After Death

> And in dying is all; and there is no other way to life and true peace.
>
> Thomas à Kempis, *The Imitation of Christ*.

There is no evidence that primates other than Man conceive of an after-life, or match the intensity of emotional distress felt by humans on the death of loved ones. Grief for the departed among the lower animals is confined, as far as we know, to a sense of deprivation of accustomed companionship, or active assistance in those day-to-day tasks requiring collaboration. In the case of a mother losing an infant, there must also be some frustration of maternal instincts that would normally have continued for as long as was necessary to ensure the baby's survival. Bewilderment, perhaps for some time biological imbalance, rather than sorrow in the human sense would be the more likely reaction of a deprived parent.

When Man began to develop his imagination, death must have acquired a much more emotional significance. Love and compassion had by now filled out the purely biological impulses that had motivated family relationships, and loss of parents and children would have been attended by that range of human sentiments we commonly associate with bereavement. Death would have assumed a religious aspect; indeed, the first archaeological evidence we possess for Man's religious beliefs has to do with his custom of burying his dead.

Some seventy thousand years ago Neanderthal man was carefully laying the bodies of his family and friends in prepared graves. In a cave near La Ferrassie in the French Dordogne, two adults and two children had been buried in shallow trenches. The man's head had been protected by stone slabs, and the woman had been tightly bound before she stiffened in *rigor mortis*, arms folded and legs pulled in tight against her trunk.

This flexing of the lower limbs seems to have been a widespread Neanderthal practice, attested from as far afield as Kiik-Koba in the Crimea, and Mount Carmel in Palestine. It has been suggested that as well as economising in the grave-digging necessary to accommodate the body, the custom may have had some cultic significance: the dead person was arranged in the foetal position he would have assumed before birth. Thus lain to rest in the womb of Mother Earth, the dead person would be symbolically prepared for rebirth. Others have preferred to think that binding the body at death meant no more than that the spirit was thereby restrained, to prevent its returning to harass the living. But in any case, the care taken at the interment indicates some considerable speculation about death and its meaning.

Burial is a religious ritual, a symbolic act whose repetition was meant to reinforce some firmly held belief not susceptible to practical demonstration. The Neanderthaler had never actually *seen* his dead relative return from the grave in the flesh, although he may have imagined his presence in a dream; yet he was so convinced that death was but a phase in the life-cycle, and that some element of the dead person would survive, that he went to the considerable trouble of safeguarding the body from marauding animals and the elements, and of ensuring that the deceased was equipped with the means of hunting and subsistence in his stage of existence. In a cemetery of ten graves scooped out of a cave-floor at Mugharet-es-Skhul on Mount Carmel, a man of about forty-five had been provided with two broken pieces of the lower jaw of a wild boar for use as weapons or implements. A youth of fifteen or sixteen had been carefully laid to rest in a cave at Le Moustier in France, with a beautifully worked stone axe by his hand. Around him, the charred bones of a prehistoric ox spoke of some funerary feast, a share of which the youth was apparently expected to take with him on his journey into the nether world. Nearby was another cave in which were found the remains of a small, possibly still-born infant; even there flint tools had been deposited alongside the corpse, perhaps on the assumption that the after-life included some possibility of growth to man's estate.

Other symbols of a continuing life were laid with the deceased in later times, such as red ochreous powder strewn on the floor of the grave or painted on the bones. This was clearly meant to represent blood, as the cowrie shells often placed with the body symbolised the gateway of life through their similarity in shape to the female vulva. There are also less easily interpreted cultic symbols, such as the circle of five or six pairs of goat horns, still attached to their parent skulls, and thrust point-down into the earth around the head of a Neanderthal child's shallow grave in eastern Uzbekistan. We can only presume the existence there of some goat cult, perhaps connected with the idea of fertility with which that animal has been traditionally associated.

All such tokens of fecundity and continuing life are in flat contradiction to the plain fact of the death they commemorate. Whence came this extraordinary willingness to look beyond observed phenomena, to reject the evidence of the senses and assert by formalised ritual the precise opposite? Was it merely wishful thinking, or sheer egotism in refusing to believe that so advanced a primate as Man, or near-Man, could perish like so much rotting vegetation? Certainly, the Neanderthaler must have been possessed of considerable self-confidence that could enable him to accept the challenge of life in the climatic conditions prevailing during the European Ice Age. But it seems at least doubtful that his achievements at bare survival would have led him to so arrogant an opinion of himself, in the face of the superior strength, speed, and adaptability of the animals he hunted, and of the remorseless powers of nature that could sweep away his puny life in a moment. It is more likely that this deep, and seemingly irrational, belief that death was not the end stemmed from an understanding and sympathy with the natural processes that were instinctive rather than intellectual. Primitive man must have sensed the truth of life's continual renewal through some genetically derived animal awareness, as the swallow knows the time for migrating, and the salmon the season and place for spawning. Even now we have not entirely lost this sense of seasonal empathy as we rejoice with the appearance of spring in the fields and hedgerows, and cannot resist the melancholy of autumn despite the breathtaking beauty of its dying leaves. The ritual of interment itself seems to be no more than the expression of a long-standing belief that death was but a prelude to new life. The flesh of the deceased, like the organic remains of all living matter, dissolves back into the earth, and is there revitalised and given fresh substance, as the womb creates new life from existing elements.

The idea that the earth is some vast primeval matrix, engendering all terrestrial life, must be very old indeed (see Chapter Twelve). It certainly goes back to the beginnings of agriculture, some ten thousand years ago. But twenty millennia before that, Old Stone Age man had tried to express his sense of kinship with Mother Earth through his wonderful cave paintings executed deep inside hillsides, far from the haunts of man. Some part of his inspiration must therefore have come from his feelings of affinity with the earth that had given his animal subjects their life and sustenance.

However much the change to a hunting economy may have disrupted primitive Man's relationship with other species, he would never have lost his understanding of the common heritage he shared with those creatures he portrayed in so lively a fashion. The blood he spilt was, in a sense, *his* blood; it was the same life-force that motivated all. It is possible that the taking of life was regarded even in Palaeolithic times as sacrificial, requiring some kind of atonement to Mother Nature for the loss of her offspring. In this case, it may well be that the representation of hunting scenes on rock-faces was a religious act, accomplished with extraordinary care and piety. For very often the pictures were executed many hundreds of yards underground, far from the light of day, and in places high above the floor of the cave. The discomfort that the artists and their assistants must have suffered was the measure of their dedication. Perhaps down there, isolated from the world of day-to-day existence, they heard the echo of the Earth-goddess's heartbeat in their own pulse, and re-experienced in the subterranean chamber something of the warm security they had once known in their mother's womb.

The Palaeolithic cave-galleries would also have seemed fitting places for the rituals accompanying adolescent initiation into manhood. In more modern aboriginal cave-sanctuaries in Australia, there are engravings on the gallery-walls which we know were shown to initiates as aids and explanations for the teachings of the tribal myths. It may well be, therefore, that in such ancient Stone Age sites as the cave at Le Tuc d'Audoubert in France, the child-size heel-prints still visible impressed into the clay floor indicate some kind of initiation dance or procession. The famous engraving on the walls of the 'Three Brothers' cave in the French Pyrenees, reputedly depicting a shaman dressed in antler headgear and a reindeer skin, may represent the dance-leader of such a mystic ceremony.

Having arrived at the bio-psychological basis of a religious sentiment like the care of the dead, it is instructive to see how its subsequent rationalisation can sometimes produce a mythology quite at variance with the original motivation. This can be serious when formalisers of a faith distort primary intuitive perceptions expressed in popular nature myths, in order to fit them into some convenient philosophic system of a more rational age. A dominant ecclesiastical hierarchy can then impose dogma on the faithful which lack any experimental support, but which might be quite powerful enough psychologically to affect attitudes of mind, and even cause severe mental trauma.

The emotionally sensitive subjects of death and the after-life are particularly vulnerable to this kind of dangerous theological restructuring. They have always exerted a powerful fascination on Man's imagination and are almost impossible to approach dispassionately. But if, as we have suggested, early Man viewed death only as a temporary interruption in the life-cycle, its contemplation is hardly likely to have engendered the terror that is so common a feature of some more organised regions. What has given death its sting is the fear of an ensuing judgment and punishment from an avenging deity. Faiths like Christianity and Islam that have traditionally associated belief with morality, portray their god as a righteous judge of souls, and the after-life as a clearing-house of moral debts. In this way the systematic theologian has found a ready solution to the age-old problem of undeserved pain, that in a world supposedly ruled by a just god, the wicked appear to flourish and the innocent suffer. The idea that life does not end at the grave offers an intellectually attractive answer: everyone receives his just deserts in the life to come, the upright to rejoice in the due reward of eternal bliss, and the guilty pay the price in dreadful retribution.

However well this neat solution may seem to balance the theologian's books, it introduced into the concept of death an element of fear that had no necessary part in the old fertility philosophy. Now the dead no longer return directly to Mother Earth's womb, to be recharged with life and born again to perpetuate the natural order. The old myth offered comfort to the dying man, and the reassurance that his life's work had not been in vain; the good that he had done would live on, to be shared and fulfilled by later generations. But death that is merely the threshold to a judgment chamber, and possibly the fires of hell, is a fearsome prospect that he may well tremble to contemplate, and which his loved ones at the graveside will shrink from acknowledging in their uncertainty of the dead man's fate before the supreme Arbiter.

Even the glorious conception of the regenerative fires that for ever burn in the heart of the earth, kindling fresh life into decaying flesh, has been corrupted by this perversion of the old myth. For now that warmth of creative mother-love has become the furnaces in the torture-chamber of a cruel god, exacting vengeance for the trangression of his laws. Pluto, the subterranean god of riches and abundance, has become the dark custodian of Hades.

Other, less ethically-orientated systems of religious belief preserve something of the primitive concept in the doctrine of rebirth and reincarnation. For example, in India such pre-Aryan ideas reassert themselves towards the end of the Vedic period (*c.* 1500–900 BC), in the assertion that after death the individual is reborn to some different form of life on earth. This continuing cycle of death and reincarnation, called *samsara*, goes on until the individual manages to overcome the gravitational pull upon himself (*karma*), and soars to freedom from all earthly existence to the peaceful isolation of *nirvana*, far beyond the concern of gods and men. The way to this liberation is by austerity, and the mental and physical disciplines of *yoga*, or 'yoking', of these energies to mystic contemplation. This negative world-view is shared by the 'heresies' of Buddhism and Jainism (6th century BC), but is also apparent in the writings of the Hindu Upanishads (8th–5th centuries, BC).

In a world-negating philosophy, 'hell', the place of punishment, is not an underworld torture-chamber, but earthly existence itself, and sin is not so much transgression of some divine moral law as spiritual ignorance, a lack of saving knowledge. The individual who fails to escape from his *karma* is a 'fool' in the biblical sense of religious obtuseness: he lacks that mystical experience that convinces the wise man of spiritual realities. The object of the yogi is to attain that knowledgeable state, a gnosis, or special understanding, which even the gods fear, for it gives the subject the secret of immortality. Whatever the psychological process that brings about this sense of omniscience and detachment, it is not achieved by concentrating the will upon a beneficent creator-god, as is the case with the Christian and Muslim mystic, but by a rigorous process of self-examination, ending, if successful, in a sublime experience of pure joy, the 'heaven' of which terrestrial suffering is the direct opposite.

The follower of the Buddha will find in the history of his master's attainment of *nirvana* the recorded pattern for his own progress. Gautama says that he knew even before his birth that the time had come for him to descend from heaven and be born into the world to preach salvation. His incarnation was in the womb of Queen Maya around the year 563 BC, in the land now known as Nepal. Shielded at first by his aristocratic upbringing from earthly trials, he nevertheless became acquainted with human suffering and resolved to discover its cure. He tried asceticism and various forms of physical mortification, but of themselves they could not bring about the release he sought, nor could he find satisfaction at the feet of his religious teachers. He then abandoned his self-imposed severities and put himself into a trance. In the first watch of the night he managed to recall from some deep level of his unconscious a memory of former incarnations. In the second watch, he attained a clarity of understanding that enabled him to survey the entire world, and see its people's sufferings and misfortunes for what they were: the result of mortal misdemeanours in their former lives. At the beginning of the third watch, a deeper appreciation of the power and tenacity of *karma* was vouchsafed him, and he passed through the eight stages of meditation (*dhyana*). He had now reached perfection, and was conscious of having come the way of all great seers who before him had achieved an understanding of eternal truth. At that moment, we are told, all heaven sang for joy, for Gautama had become the Buddha, the 'Enlightened One', and could now, through his own insight, lead others to escape from the 'purgatory' of living to *nirvana,* and thus free themselves from the weary cycle of continual reincarnation.

The way to salvation, Buddha taught, lies within Man himself. The bondage of *karma* that keeps him within the gravitational orbit of rebirth is fuelled by Man's own craving to exist; let him extirpate this desire by self-discipline of mind and body, and he will break out of the cycle, the flame of self-perpetuation will be extinguished, and he will have attained *nirvana.*

The ideas of reincarnation, *karma,* and *nirvana,* were not original to Buddha, but were generally current in his day. His contribution was to bring to these age-old concepts a combination of mysticism and philosophic inquiry. He was concerned not only with the attainment of the self's liberation, but with helping others to defeat the power of *karma* that held their souls in bondage. Since this will to exist was dependent upon the manner of people's lives in their successive incarnations, he addressed himself also to such problems as free-will and determinism, and the relationship of cause and effect in the empirical world.

It is not difficult to appreciate how such a world-negating attitude can develop in a country like India, where natural disasters can suddenly turn a land of tropical luxuriance into a flood-swept swamp or a parched wilderness that cannot sustain the abundant life it had hitherto encouraged. Nevertheless, in biological terms the wish to extinguish the flame of survival is a curious phenomenon. It is difficult to believe that the European Neanderthaler, who took such pains to ensure that some element of his dead relations should survive, endured fewer hardships out there on the fringes of the ice sheets than the Indian peasant in his treacherous river-valleys. Yet one cannot doubt that primitive Man's acceptance of the challenge of suffering achieved the continuance and development of the human race. Perhaps the difference in outlook has to do with the fact that the ecological conditions of the Ice Age did not permit of the proliferation of the human species to the extent fostered periodically in the alluvial plains of India. Neanderthal man and his evolutionary successors were not therefore subjected to the stresses of over-population, whose effect upon the living organism, animal and human, we are only now beginning to appreciate. Experience has shown all too clearly that overcrowded conditions can generate aggressive tendencies which, if they cannot for social reasons be turned outwards against our neighbours, find their outlet in a death-wish within ourselves. It is almost as though Man carries a biological 'self-destruct' mechanism that comes automatically into operation when his numbers reach an optimum consistent with efficient survival in a limited natural economy. Wars, and other organised genocidal activities, are more deliberate expressions of this self-limiting mechanism; less conscious, perhaps, is a psychological readiness to abandon the will to survive in a hostile environment. Small wonder that our disillusioned young people escape from a claustrophobic urban civilisation and seek the way to *nirvana* at the feet of an eastern guru.

One interesting innovation that Buddha brought into the concept of rebirth was a denial that it entailed the plurality of souls, suggesting that even Heaven by now must be overcrowded. The individual did not survive death; it was merely the craving for life activating the will of the dying man that endured. Should he have overcome this desire and subdued his *karma*, there would be no rebirth. The idea was a break from the understanding current at his time and persisting into later Hinduism, that there was some permanent element in each man's personality that was reincarnated at successive rebirths, a concept more akin to the idea of the individual soul that we find in Greek and Christian philosophy. For Buddha, nothing was permanent except *nirvana*; the soul is but a complex series of short-lived states or events, and has no reality outside the peculiar circumstances realised in this mortal existence. Thus the idea of reincarnation as a transmigration of individual and unchangeable elements from one psychophysical organism to another is untenable. The question asked of Jesus in the New Testament story about marriage relationships in heaven reflecting earthly circumstances: 'If a man's brother die, and leave a wife behind him, and leave no child, that his brother should take his wife and raise up seed to his brother . . . .', and so on (Mark 12: 18–23), would have had no more meaning to the Buddha than the kind of Jewish angelology assumed in the Nazarene teacher's reply: 'For when they shall rise from the dead, they neither marry, nor are given in marriage; but they are as angels in heaven' (v. 25).

In some respects, this impersonal aspect of Gautama's understanding of rebirth reflects the primitive idea of life after death. For surely it was this urge to exist, so deplored by the Buddha, that the Neanderthal mourner hoped his funerary rites might help to perpetuate. This was the precious spark that would accompany the rotting corpse of his dear friend to the womb of Mother Earth; it was this desire for life that would be rekindled into a new organism and born again to continue the natural cycle.

9

The Sanctity of Life

When he began hunting animals of his own size and larger, the evolving primate necessarily alienated himself to some extent from his fellow-creatures. He would always maintain a deep empathy with the rest of the animal world, thanks to a common biological heritage. Nevertheless, his very success in the hunt must create a division between 'them' and 'us'; they are the prey, and we their hunters and superiors. When Man's children began making pets of young animals taken from their lairs, possibly the origin of animal domestication, that sense of superiority, and the idea that the rest of the living world exists primarily to serve Man, was given fresh impetus. This is the beginning of an anthropocentric philosophy of nature and it persisted into those religions which envisage the creator-god as a kind of Superman, making humans in His own image.

Most animals in the wild have natural allies whose instinctive reactions to danger they are pleased to share at times of greater risk. Thus baboons and impala often feed together on the African savannahs and mutually profit from each other's special aptitudes: the baboon's visual powers supplement the impala's keen sense of smell. Each can react swiftly enough on its own, but together they are almost immune to the danger of sudden attacks from their common foes, the lions and other big cats. When Man became a 'mighty Nimrod', his quarries learnt to class him as an enemy, more dangerous by his skills and cunning than the predators his ancestors once helped them evade.

We may see here the origins of that strange love–hate relationship that persists between Man and other animals. We have never quite lost that feeling of guilt that our primate ancestors incurred when first they spilt the blood of their evolutionary kin. As we shall see later, atoning for this primeval betrayal forms an essential part of religious sacrifice. It may well be that our modern humanitarian regard for animal welfare, sometimes, one feels, outweighing our concern for human beings, owes something to this same unease, and is a compensatory reaction for the contemporary weakening of religious belief and practice. Incidentally, it is an interesting side-light on human nature and our conflicting emotions that although we react violently against wanton cruelty to pets, we applaud with delighted approval the spectacle of hoop-jumping tigers and ball-balancing sea-lions in our circuses. In the degradation of their dignity we are reassured of our own superiority and reject the plain witness of our instincts that we share a common origin.

The introduction of agricultural technology some ten thousand years ago made Stone Age Man less dependent upon hunting and food-gathering, and offered him the opportunity of a more settled existence. Nowadays, our anthropologists are finding it more and more difficult to discover primitive communities for whom hunting is still the main means of sustenance, or who can still cherish in their tribal memories relics of religious belief and ritual that stem from their days as hunters. One such people are the Ainu who inhabit the islands of Hokkaido, Sakhalin, and Kurile, north of Japan. Since the colonisation of their homelands by the Japanese early in this century, the Ainu have been driven to adopt agriculture to supplement their diminishing reserves of wild game. Nevertheless, they continue to observe much of the old religion and hunting rituals of their fore-fathers, and thus serve the anthropologist still as a rich source of information about the attitude of Palaeolithic men towards the animal world.

The Ainu believe that all animals possess some measure of divine energy, or *ramat*, but that some species are more powerfully endowed than others, and may be considered as gods, or *kamui*. Of such are bears and foxes, and in certain magical situations these animals can assume human form when they will display for good or ill the character possessed by them in their original state.

Other hunting peoples similarly pay special reverence to certain species of animals, and go so far as to credit them with fathering their respective human clans when the world was young. This concept, known generally under the old Algonquin Indian word, *totem*, is characteristic also of the Australian aborigines. They claim for their various families special relationship to such animals as the bear, wolf, and snake, and among these groups the slaughter and eating of their totem ancestor is strictly forbidden, except on certain ritual occasions. Marriage partners have also generally to be chosen from some clan other than one's own, as if to marry a person descended from the same animal ancestor would be in some way incestuous.

Anthropologists find in totemism a vital source of religious belief generally, and some even claim that religion stems directly from this one concept. But whatever its place in the range of contributory factors, there can be little doubt that there lies deep in Man's genetic consciousness an awareness of his affinity with the rest of the animal world, edged with fear and guilt for the betrayal perpetrated by our forefathers when first they turned upon their natural allies for food.

In the religious customs and social manners of the East generally, this human ambivalence of attitude towards animals is particularly marked even today. Among the Hindus, the doctrine of *ahimsa*, 'non-violence', is ranked high among the virtues, expressing the sacredness of all life. The Jains, although non-deists, take it to the extreme in their precautions against harming living creatures, from human beings to microscopic organisms; even their drinking water has to be strained to avoid swallowing minute fauna, and they wear gauze masks to filter the air they breathe lest they inhale winged insects. On the other hand, as every visitor to eastern lands is well enough aware, the most appalling cruelty is inflicted daily on beasts of burden by overwork and neglect, as would not be tolerated for a moment in most western cultures.

There is also in Hinduism a more mystical reverence for the animal world that betrays itself in the old belief that dumb beasts have a special knowledge normally inaccessible to human beings. This science of *pashu-vidya,* 'animal lore', is considered essential study for anyone wishing to understand the mysteries of the universe and the manipulation of its powers for magical purposes. In essence, the idea stems from Man's appreciation that his animal cousins do indeed possess certain faculties, like senses of time and direction, that have never developed in humans or are but poorly represented. The hunter also knew that his quarry had means of communicating with others of its kind in ways that were beyond Man's comprehension, despite his own wonderful powers of speech and understanding. The mystics liked to believe that a few gifted men and women share the ability to commune with more than their own species: snake-charmers could converse with snakes, monkey-men with monkeys, while other specialists could become the confidants of scorpions, lizards, fish, or birds. One is reminded of the animal 'familiars' of the European witches who were believed to act as their intermediaries with the spirit world. The 'Devil' himself took on animal form at their Sabbaths.

The idea of communicating with animals through some special faculty is not that remote from everyday life. Devoted pet-owners are aware of a bond of understanding between them and their animals which is almost human in its sympathy, and the working partnership that the shepherd establishes with his dogs must seem to the uninitiated as mysterious as the Hindu mystic's *pashu-vidya.*

The early Buddhists and Jains built hospitals for the care of animals, birds, and even insects. The English traveller, Ralph Fitch, recording his journeys in Bengal in the sixteenth century, says:

> They have hospitals for sheep, goats, dogs, cats, birds and for all other living creatures. When they be old and lame they keep them until they die. If a man catch or buy any live thing in other places and bring it to them, they will give him money for it or other victual, and keep it in the hospitals or let it go. (Quoted by Walker, *Hindu World*, i, p. 16.)

Where killing involved the shedding of blood, it was considered particularly heinous; as the seat of life, blood was imbued with great power which would react against the perpetrator of such sacrilege. This fearsome prospect led to some strange practices. It is said that the kings of ancient Calicut used to pay priests to deflower their virgin wives lest the sin of causing pain and shedding blood should be counted against them.

Such extreme care to avoid harming a fellow-creature rests on the belief that wilful, or even unintentional destruction of life has especially serious karmic effects on the individual concerned; it must impair his chances of escape from the cycle of rebirth.

The late Mahatma Gandhi carried the doctrine of non-violence successfully into politics although there, as in many such mass movements of non-collaboration with authority, sheer weight of numbers gave his party's activities a savagely brutal force, as aggressive as the military might aligned against him. Nevertheless, Ghandi was able to draw upon a deep fount of popular sympathy at home and abroad, for the idea of avoiding injury to one's fellow-creatures runs deep in the human psyche. Dr Albert Schweitzer proclaimed the sanctity of life as the guiding inspiration of his medical missionary work in Lambaréné, and today many charitable organisations, not all of them sponsored by religious bodies, would voice similar sentiments in justification of their work among the sick and underprivileged.

The specifically Christian concern for life claims a more objective moral basis than that underlying Hindu 'non-violence'. In India, the doctrine of *ahimsa* is primarily a means of acquiring merit for oneself, reflected in the name given to charitable medical institutions, *punya-shala,* 'merit-places'. Schweitzer himself draws a distinction between the Christian ethic and Hindu motivation when he says that the latter 'does not arrive from a feeling of compassion, but from the idea of keeping oneself undefiled from the world' (*Indian Thought and Its Development*, London, 1951, p. 80).

The Church proclaims that every human being is a child of a loving God and that the care of souls is a believer's duty, quite apart from any merit that might accrue to himself. However, since the soul is not to be identified with the body in Christian tradition, the precise area of altruistic concern has posed a number of practical and doctrinal problems which have never been satisfactorily resolved. The medieval Inquisitors found nothing unethical about inflicting the most horrible tortures on the flesh of recalcitrant 'heretics', in order that their souls might be saved from worse fates in eternity. They found their moral justification authoritatively voiced by St Augustine who, centuries before, had been convinced that 'not only every pagan but every Jew, heretic, and schismatic will go to the eternal fire . . . unless before the end of his life he be reconciled and restored to the Catholic Church'. Even today, some controversy surrounds the question of what constitutes an inviolate personality in such matters of life and death as abortion: at what stage does the soul enter the foetus so that thereafter its destruction must be counted a mortal sin?

Modern humanitarian concern for the welfare of living creatures is less troubled with such theological divisions of responsibility. Like the atheistic Jain, the ecologist deals with living matter generally, vegetation as well as animals and humans. His more pragmatic ethic rests upon the recognition that Man is dependent upon the planet's natural resources for his continued existence. Unnecessary violence against living beings can be quite as harmful to the perpetrator as for the victims, at least in the long run. Depletion of wild-life leaves mankind the poorer, spiritually as well as economically.

At root here is no one religious creed but a sentiment that springs from a deep-seated awareness of Man's common heritage with all forms of life. As we noted earlier, the Stone Age artists who painted wild animals on cave walls in France and Spain showed a sympathy with their subjects which would not have tolerated killing for killing's sake. Whatever the purpose of those hunting scenes, totemic, magical, or religious, the care taken by the ancient craftsmen in their graphic studies of local fauna demonstrates not only a keen eye for line and colour, but a respect and admiration for their natural vigour. It is true that the animals depicted are all intended quarry and would serve to satisfy the hunter's bodily needs, but the artists do not represent the animals as so many joints of meat or warm skins, but as creatures vibrant with life. The blood the hunter must reluctantly shed embodied a life-force that he himself shared. He may have pitted his superior wits against his prey, but there is clear evidence that he recognised their superior powers in other respects, for he took pains to extract from his victims' bones the marrow that he believed might endow him with some of their strength, and he drew from their skulls the brain matter that he hoped might enhance his cunning.

The animal would die at the hunter's hand, but its life would be continued in the flesh of those who consumed it. Man, too, must die, and his body would feed the earth and in due course bring forth fresh life to serve the needs of his successors. So the natural process of regeneration or, in religious terms, reincarnation, would continue, and its laws must have been recognised by primitive Man from the earliest days. He would have been equally aware that natural disasters like floods and extreme climatic conditions could disrupt this process, bringing famine and suffering in their wake. Equally, Man's own tampering with the natural balance that matched consumption with supply could bring disaster. Decimate a herd beyond its abilities to recuperate and the next season's migration would bring insufficient numbers to maintain the huntsmen themselves. Later, the agriculturist would similarly learn that to exploit one plot of land continually without time to regain its strength would weaken the productivity of the soil for subsequent seasons.

There seems good reason to believe that this sense of necessary equilibrium in nature is instinctive in Man and animals. Wild creatures seldom kill more than they need for food; non-hunting aggression is usually no more than a threat to maintain social or territorial position, and such struggles for group supremacy in the wild rarely result in death. Where wanton savagery does occur, we may seek the cause in some particular stress-inducing circumstance like overcrowding or mental confusion. There again, this is not a feature of life in the wild; it is more common in the kind of restrictive conditions experienced in the zoo or laboratory. Experiments have shown that there comes a moment in controlled states of overcrowding when tension reaches such a pitch that the animals develop diseases, kill their young, and fight viciously among themselves to the death. The whole social order is disrupted, and the individual creatures are completely disorientated. In the end, deaths reach such proportions that the population is cut back to a lower density and breeding can begin again in more relaxed conditions.

Man has not yet reached such dire straits, although our ecologists warn us that it will not be long before we run out of food and living space for our ever-increasing millions. Our occasional vicious behaviour towards others of our own species often has a more immediate cause in the conflict between desire and duty in an over-regulated society. The resultant build-up of stress periodically explodes in anti-social behaviour. Man's innate sense of natural justice is swamped in a wave of unreasoning hatred and wilful destruction that can include killing for its own sake. However, that does not prevent him assuming as a matter of course that Nature will normally act in a more balanced fashion. He expects a dearth one year to be followed by a bumper harvest the next, that a perfect summer will have to be 'paid for' with a cruel winter following, that births will normally be matched with deaths, female babies with males, and so on. And he projects this instinctive understanding of natural 'fairplay' into a religious conception of a just God, who requires of his people a similar equilibrium in society, giving as well as taking, recognising the rights of others, and generally observing the sanctity of life.

10

Blood Sacrifice

To help him in his primeval struggle against the forces of evil, Mithras, the Iranian solar deity, sacrificed a mighty bull. It was a creative and redemptive act, for the animal symbolised the natural world. From its stricken side flowed corn and vines, the fruits of an earth now made for ever fertile. Thereafter, the Mithraic worshipper celebrated the event with a similar offering at the altar, and with a commemorative meal of bread and wine when he looked forward to the final sacrifice by the great god. When the last animal died at his hands, it would give men not merely the food of life on earth, but immortality.

At the heart of this myth there lies the intuitive awareness that death is a necessary prelude to new life, and that some kind of sacrifice must be involved if the cycle of rebirth is to be perpetuated. In appropriating the earth's gifts to his own use, Man upsets the balance of nature, and has to make some token restoration. This basic concept has been elaborated and variously expressed in all the great religions of mankind but the sense of Man's indebtedness to nature lies deeper than any theological speculation. We feel some perpetual unease that through our very existence on the planet we incur a debt with something or somebody which we can only resolve by giving back an earnest of good faith. It may be no more than a gesture of thanksgiving before meals, or setting aside a choice morsel of food as a preliminary offering to a tutelary deity. The sacrifice may, however, be of a more considerable nature, involving real self-denial. The suppliant removes from common usage some prized possession, like the first-fruits of field, flocks, or even of his wife's womb. In the last resort he will frustrate that most fundamental instinct of self-preservation and sacrifice his own well-being and life itself. In religious terms, Man tries to atone for his 'sin', that is, at root, his seizure of the fruits of divine grace without proper regard to the needs of natural justice, and thus seeks to maintain a right relationship with his god.

We see this principle of compensatory atonement most clearly in the rituals that traditionally accompanied the gathering of especially sacred herbs or drug-plants. The best-known of these was, of course, the Mandrake, whose reputed power over a man's mind was partly attributable to its supposed human shape. The name came to be applied to a number of different roots thought to bear some resemblance to a part of the body, but, as we have shown elsewhere, the original Mandrake was probably that narcotic fungus known as Flyagaric, or the *Amanita muscaria* (*The Sacred Mushroom and the Cross*, London, 1970, p. 41). This red-and-white topped mushroom, whose phallic shape prompted its anthropomorphic reputation, has been known and revered from the earliest times, and has, through its distinctive colouring and form, inspired a wealth of folklore the world over. In religious circles it has been particularly prized for its hallucinatory effects, derived from a poison concealed under the 'warts' on its cap. Even today, this and similarly endowed fungi are used as part of the stimulatory apparatus of shamans and other ecstatic visionaries in South America and elsewhere.

Recently, scholars have suggested that it is this mushroom that was the original *Soma*, that mysterious drug-plant celebrated in the Hindu Rig-veda. It was said to have been the source of Indra's great power and all his mighty deeds. It was known as the 'King of Plants', and conferred vitality, immortality and inspiration upon all who drank of its juice. It was deified as 'everlasting, omnipotent, all-healing, the bestower of riches, and giver of immortality'. The whole of the ninth book of the Rig-veda is devoted to its praise: 'Where there is eternal radiance, where life is free, where there is desire and delight, where joy and pleasure abide, there, O Soma, make me immortal.'

The sacred plant has much in common in its reputed attributes with the *Nectar* of the Greek legends, 'the food of the gods', and may, indeed, be similarly identified. Certainly, Soma has an equivalent in the sacred herb of the Persian Avesta, the *Haoma,* venerated there as 'Son of the Great God, Ahura Mazda'.

The Soma rite in Hinduism was chiefly concerned with the extraction and preparation of the powerful juice, for it served not only as a hallucinatory potion for the priests, but as a sacrificial libation to the gods; indeed, it formed the basis of the Rig-vedic sacrificial system. As might be expected, the gathering of such powerful herbs as this was thought to be attended by severe hazard; the collector was, after all, robbing Mother Earth of one of her most precious children. It had been engendered, like all vegetation, by the storm-god, whose semen was ejaculated as rain upon the open vulva of the Earth-goddess (see Chapter Twelve). But in the case of the phallic Mandrake, the 'Holy Plant', as it was called, its shape more perfectly represented its divine progenitor than any other herb and so was credited with bearing within it the god's seed in a uniquely powerful form.

Small wonder, then, that cautionary tales abounded about its uprooting. One of the most common was the suggestion that some animal should be employed to take the risk of snatching the Mandrake from the ground. We are advised, for instance, to tie a dog to the root and then call the poor beast from a distance. When it springs to obey, the Mandrake will be dragged screaming from the soil. The dog will immediately die, but its vicarious death will allow the gatherer thereafter to handle the dangerous herb with impunity.

Of more interest from our immediate point of view

are the traditions that require some kind of restitution to be made to Mother Earth for the loss of this and similarly prized herbs. As Pliny the Elder (AD 23–79) says of the plant Asclepius, possibly another name for the sacred fungus: 'it is a pious duty to fill in the hole with cereals as an atonement to the earth' (*Natural History*, XXV, 30). Josephus, the first-century Jewish historian, warns the gatherer of the Mandrake that 'to touch it is fatal unless one succeeds in bringing along the thing itself, that is, the root, hanging from one's hand' (*War*, VII, 181).

This tradition implies that a replacement or substitution of the Mandrake had to be offered, but, since both must come ultimately from God, the imbalance involved in its rape from the earth remains unresolved. A fourteenth-century BC liturgist from Bronze Age Ugarit in ancient Syria had long before called upon the great fertility god Baal for help in this problem of compensation:

> The message of the Mighty Baal, the word of the Womb-favourer: Put bread into the ground, set Mandrakes in the dust, pour a compensatory offering in the midst of the earth, a peace offering in the midst of the fields! ('*nt* III, 10–14.)

The idea here expressed is that the magic plant is so god-like in its power that only a substitute provided by the deity himself can adequately atone for its plunder. Similarly, the deified Soma in the Rig-veda is sacrificially crushed to provide the means of achieving immortality for his votaries, and the divinely-engendered Haoma of the Avesta is pounded in a mortar to bestow life sacramentally upon the worshippers of Ahura Mazda, his heavenly father. There is a parallel in the Christian belief that God sent his Son Jesus in human form to be offered as a sacrifice to atone for Man's sin.

Propitiatory self-sacrifice by the deity is a common feature of agrarian mythology, and its cultic expression often took the form of human sacrifice. The victim was identified with the god and then slaughtered and dismembered. His broken flesh was scattered upon the fields, symbolising the god's seed, rain, which fecundates Mother Earth. The human being thus devoted has of recent times been almost universally replaced by some more humanely acceptable substitute such as animal, or part of the vegetation itself. However, human sacrifice is said to have been practised by the Khonds of Bengal until comparatively recently. They are one of the aboriginal tribes of India who, like other so-called Kolarian peoples, entered the sub-continent in prehistoric times. Their sacrificial victim, called the *meriah*, offered himself voluntarily for the ordeal, and was himself born of parents who had fulfilled the role. He was purchased by the community and thereafter allowed to live normally for several years. He could marry and have children until such time as it was deemed opportune for his immolation. Then, following a communal orgy, the *meriah* was consecrated as the incarnation of the deity and worshipped with chanting and dancing. The devotees prayed thus to their goddess: 'O Goddess, we offer thee this sacrifice; give us good harvests, good seasons, and good health!'

The guilt that might have lain heavy upon their consciences through the killing of another human being was assuaged in the knowledge that he had volunteered for the office of *meriah*, and had been paid for his services by the community. They were able therefore to turn to the victim at this time and say: 'We have bought thee and have not seized thee by force; now we sacrifice thee, and may no sin be accounted to us!'

After being drugged with opium, the man was strangled. His body was cut into pieces and distributed around the villages, each community burying their fragment of the flesh in a field. The remainder of the body was burnt and the ashes strewn over the land. After the British had suppressed the practice, a goat or buffalo was substituted for the human *meriah*, but clearly the rite's central feature was the devotion of a victim who could, in the eyes of the assembled company, more adequately represent an anthropomorphic deity. A parallel to this sacrifice may perhaps be detected in the ritual breaking of the body of the Vedic creator-god Prajapati ('creation-king'), father of all living things, whose cultus vitalises and sustains all life.

Among Mexican farmers in Aztec times, maize was the staple crop and accordingly featured as the focus of their religion. The maize plant was deified in the person of Cinteotl, whose power resided in the foodstuff, nurtured by Mother Earth. Tradition told how the god loved the pretty but flirtatious mistress of the rain-god Tlaloc, so in ritual the personification of the maize in its various stages of growth was undertaken by the young women of the community. When the first green ears appeared, the girls took some and danced with their hair thrown loose and their breasts exposed. They brought back a shoot, representing their god, in procession to the temple of Chicomecoatl, the goddess of sustenance. Gathered there was a group of young girls of different ages, denoting the maize-plant's growth. Three months later, when the crop was ripe, one of the young women, consecrated as the manifestation of the goddess of new maize, Xilonen, was ritually beheaded. This marked the freeing of the crop for use by the whole community as food, much as the offering of the first-fruits in ancient Israel signalled the secularisation of the harvests (Exodus 22:29; 23:16, 19; etc.).

Sixty days later, at the conclusion of the harvest, there was another human sacrifice. This time a woman representing the goddess Toci, 'Our Mother', deity of the gathered maize, was beheaded and her body immediately flayed. One priest arrayed himself in the skin, while a piece taken from the thigh was carried to the temple of Cinteotl, the Maize god, where another devotee laid it upon his face as a mask. In this guise he assumed the role of a woman in childbirth, symbolising the rebirth of the 'dead' Toci, in anticipation of the following season's germination of the dried seed-corn.

Each Aztec town or village held its own sacrificial ceremonies to the various gods and goddesses of their pantheon. The victims were mostly prisoners-of-war, but when this supply fell short, slaves and children were bought to ensure a constant source of re-invigoration for the gods. Each of the eighteen months of the Aztec year had its religious festival, and the ceremonies were devised to suit the nature of the deity being honoured. In the case of the fertility god Xipe Totec ('Our Lord of the Flayed One'), often portrayed wearing a flayed human skin to symbolise the fresh covering of spring vegetation, the prisoners were crucified above the ground and shot to death with arrows. Their blood dripped onto the ground beneath, representing the life-giving rain on which the parched earth depended for its fertility.

The sacrifice performed in honour of Tezcatlipoca ('Smoking Mirror'), god of the night sky and patron deity of young warriors, the elite of Aztec society, is another example of the victim being substituted for the god himself. The commemorative feast fell in the fifth month, but preparations began a full year beforehand, when the priests chose a young man from among their captives to be the divine incarnation. He must be without blemish, and in every way worthy of the image of the god. He was taught to behave like a nobleman, and for that year he was accorded the honours of a lord, as the living representative of his divine patron. He was taught to play the flute, and given an entourage of eight attendants who accompanied him everywhere, waiting upon his every whim. He was dressed in rich clothes, bedecked with gold jewellery, and spent his time in pleasurable pursuits, strolling through the city with a tobacco pipe in his hand, and garlanded with flowers. Twenty days before the festival, the incarnate god was married to four young women. With just five days to go, his dress and hair style were changed to those of a war chief, and he spent the remainder of his time feasting, singing, and dancing in various parts of the city.

On the day of the feast, his wives and attendants accompanied him by canoe to a small temple on the lake shore. There the women bade him a tender farewell, and he walked to the temple pyramid along with his male companions. At this point, they, too, departed, leaving him to climb the great staircase quite alone, breaking one of his clay flutes he had played during his year of office at each step. Above him stood the priest-executioners, waiting. When he reached them, they seized him, spread-eagled him face upwards over a low stone block, and held him down by his arms and legs. A fifth priest held his head back; another raised the ceremonial knife, and with a single stroke cut through the youth's ribs and breastbone. The priest thrust a hand through the gaping wound and wrenched out the victim's heart, still pulsing with its life-blood, and held it up to the sun in grateful adoration. The god had provided and now received himself back, a full and perfect sacrifice for his own people.

In such a militaristic society, the cult of blood-sacrifice takes on a special significance and, among the Aztecs, reached horrific proportions. Their chief deity was the sun-god Huitzilopochtli, whose daily renewal was thought to depend upon a constant supply of human blood. Each night he had to contend with the forces of darkness, and the sacrifices were intended to sustain him in his struggle, and to ensure his reappearance the following day.

In the year 1487, when the god's great temple was dedicated, it is said that twenty thousand captives were killed in his honour and their hearts offered at the altar. The victims stood waiting their turn to be sacrificed in a four-lane queue that stretched for two miles through the city.

Whatever the philosophic and cultic justification for

these blood-baths, the observer must wonder at the compulsive power of a religion that makes ordinary, otherwise rational human beings behave towards their fellow-men in such an unnatural way. Bearing in mind what we have earlier said about Man's inclination to value life as sacred, how, we may ask, can he be persuaded, like the Aztecs, to condemn to death some ten to fifteen thousand people annually, to secure some advantage from gods whose very existence must be a matter of conjecture? Of course, fear must be counted a major factor in religious attitudes; the Aztecs had been led by their teachers to believe that failure to feed the gods with human blood would prejudice their own survival. Then, again, the majority of the victims would have been captives taken in battle from other tribes or races; their deaths would not have been so emotively disturbing as the sacrifice of close relations. On the other hand, the young women who were annually beheaded to promote the success of the maize crop were presumably daughters of the farmers themselves, and we need not doubt that their loss was as heart-breaking to their families as the more legendary sacrifice of Jephthah's only child, in the Old Testament agrarian myth (Judges 11:30–40).

Some idea of the degree of compulsion that motivated human sacrifice may be judged from the following account left to us by an eye-witness of the sixteenth century. The Spanish priests who accompanied the Conquistadores had made it their mission to bring the Christian faith to the Maya of Yucatán. Not surprisingly, their 'conversion' was at best tenuous, and for decades after the arrival of the Spaniards there was a good deal of backsliding among the converts that gave the missionaries much cause for concern.

One such relapse into paganism was witnessed by a young converted schoolmaster, Juan Couoh, and reported by him to his religious superiors. Juan himself seems to have been torn in his mind between his new religion and the more deeply-ingrained faith of his forefathers. He admitted to having kept in hiding in a cave about sixty idols that had belonged to his father, and to having made offerings to them at various times. He also confessed to having been present at a ritual in a church during which a deer and some turtles were offered to the Maya deities. The incident he then went on to relate was rather more serious.

I was in my house one Tuesday evening [he testified] when at midnight Diego Pech, the cacique of Yaxcaba, sent for me to read a letter for him. On my way there, I passed by the church where I saw Pedro Euan, principal of Yaxcaba, who in ancient times had the office of sacrificing men and boys to idols. He had a youngster from Tekax, in the province of Mani, with his hands tied behind his back. This boy, Francisco Cauich, had gone on holiday to Yaxcaba to visit some relatives who lived there. He was seated next to the pedestal of the altar in the church. . . .

In front they laid a large mat, and on top of it they placed a flint knife with its handle wrapped in a white cloth. Then Gaspar Chim and Pedro Pech, former pagan priests, took two candles, and all sat down on stools. They ordered the Indian seated by the altar to be brought, and they seated him in their midst. His hands were tied, his eyes were covered with a cloth, and he wore no shirt, only short drawers. Gaspar Chim said that I would tell the friars about this, and under the threat of being myself sacrificed, I promised not to tell what I saw. Then Diego Pech said to the youth whom they were going to sacrifice, and who was weeping, 'Be of good heart; don't be upset. We're not going to harm you. We're not sending you to hell, but to glory in the sky, as our ancestors used to do.'

'Do as you will', the boy replied; 'God who is in heaven will help me.'

Then Gaspar Chim said, 'Untie him and do what must be done before it dawns and people are around.'

They untied the youngster and threw him on the mat. The priests handed over the candles they were holding, and four of them caught hold of the boy and placed him in a prone position, holding him by his hands and feet. Pedro Euan, taking the flint knife, made an opening on the left side of the youth's heart, grasped the heart and cut the arteries with the knife. He gave the severed heart to the priest, Gaspar Chim, who made two cuts like a cross in its extremity and then raised it on high. Next he took some part – I don't know which it was – and placed it in the mouth of the largest of the idols, which was that of Itzamna. Then he took the boy's body and heart, with the blood they had collected in a large gourd, along with the idols, and all went with them to the cacique's house. I don't know what they did there. As they left, they again warned me not to speak to the friars of what I had seen. They added, 'Even if they burn us alive, we must not say a word.'

I went to my house, for what they had done seemed very evil. (From a translation by Eric Thompson in *Rise and Fall of Maya Civilisation*, 1954, p. 243f.)

Doubtless the punitive burnings that almost certainly followed this damning testimony were regarded by the miscreants and most of their compatriots as being no less religiously motivated than their own ritual murder of the boy. The Christians, they would think, were merely appeasing their god by sacrificing the priests in an effort to offset the merit earned with the Maya deities through the offering of the boy's heart and blood. It would hardly have been counted a moral issue of right and wrong. The Maya priests had obeyed the dictates of their consciences, conditioned by centuries of religious tradition which was far more deeply engrained than any new-fangled cult imported from abroad and disseminated under the persuasive power of the conqueror's sword. For the priests to have compromised their faith, even at the stake, would have been a far more heinous sin in their eyes than prematurely ending the life of an innocent lad visiting his kinsfolk on holiday.

Cultic sin extends over many fields of human behaviour. The divinely-ordained laws transgressed may relate to social affinities, such as those forbidding marriage between totem-related clans, or incestuous alliances, or to other deeply-rooted taboos like avoiding menstrual blood, women in childbirth, or dead bodies. To the casual observer, many of the inhibitions must seem trivial and hardly worth the precautions taken against their infringement, or the sacrifices made by the subject for their atonement. Nevertheless, religious guilt can weigh more heavily upon the conscience of a believer than a sceptic can fully understand, for the religionist's mind has been conditioned by tribal traditions, if not genetic inheritance, to regard such taboos and inhibitions as mandatory.

We saw above that submission to religiously-inspired laws has given Man a stability that the shifting sands of technical progress and political change might otherwise have denied him. The price he has paid has been an over-sensitive religious conscience that has driven people to commit outrageous acts of violence against their fellow-men in the name of their gods. On a less drastic level than human sacrifice, but nonetheless as morally abhorrent, are those physical and psychological assaults perpetrated on young people during adolescent initiation rituals to fit them to take their submissive place in society (see Chapter Seven). Such 'instant' reorientation of young minds might be justified on grounds of exigence in the case of hard-pressed communities, but the wider application of religious pressures to induce whole classes or races of people to accept perpetually subordinate roles as their divinely-ordained duty, savours of political exploitation that does not even have the biological necessity of primate baboonism to support it.

Yet, however much the observer may deplore the masochistic lengths to which pious obedience can drive the believer, it has to be acknowledged that the mental torment of a religious person who feels himself estranged from his god through some real or fancied breach of sacred duty is genuine enough. In an effort to alleviate his condition, the 'sinner' will unmercifully punish not only himself, but his fellow-creatures, flouting the most basic laws of self-preservation, and every inherited instinct for natural justice.

Religious guilt is but one of the stresses to which *Homo sapiens* is subject, and stress of any kind gives rise to aggression. We should therefore seek the psychological motivation for extreme forms of penitence in the normal, aggressive reactions of our evolutionary forebears turned inwards upon ourselves. Redirected aggression is well known to students of animal behaviour as an instinctive response to the frustrations of dominance rivalry. When two equally strong contestants for leadership meet head-on, and are afraid to attack each other, they will often redirect their frustrated violence onto some weaker animal that has the misfortune to be in the vicinity at the time of the clash. In the restricted circumstances of zoos and laboratories, animals under stress are apt to turn this aggression upon themselves, and have been known to bite their own flesh to the bone in their frustration at being unable to attack their enemies on the other side of the cage bars. *Homo sapiens* alone in the animal world takes this self-directed aggression to the extreme of committing suicide, but the underlying causes for such tragedies can usually be traced to the same kind of tension operating in a dominance-orientated society. The underdog, unable to work off his grievances on his superiors, will turn on his inferiors, if not at work, at home – on his wife, his family, or even the household pets. In the last resort he will do away with himself, and hope by this final, despairing gesture, to inflict more humiliation upon an unsympathetic world than he could ever do through face-to-face confrontation.

Religious man has even greater frustrations to contend with. As well as being aware of the social pressures that require him to subordinate his own immediate desires to the long-term interests of the community, he must further acknowledge his obligations to God, and the need to expiate his sins. He stands in constant debt to nature for his predatory expropriation of the earth's riches, and, try as he may, he will inevitably at some time break the taboos that regulate his existence and determine his relationships with a capricious deity.

Religion, however, also offers its believers an outlet

for their repressed emotion in the ritual of sacrifice, either of themselves in self-punishment penitence, or, less dangerously for the future of the species, of some prized possession. So, whatever its philosophical justification, religious sacrifice has a subjective, therapeutic value. In his blood offerings, Man has found emotional relief for his frustrated impulses. He has not only been able to relieve his conscience by making some token retribution to his god by offering back the essence of the victim's life, but he has found an acceptable means of compensating for his own inadequacy through redirected aggression.

An example of some such group-therapy may be seen in the ceremony of the Scapegoat observed annually by the ancient Israelites. During the ritual, they unloaded their sins metaphorically onto the back of a sacrificial goat, and then drove it to a violent death in the wilderness. A second animal they slaughtered and sprinkled its blood on Yahweh's altar (Leviticus 16). It is not difficult to imagine the emotions aroused by such cathartic rituals performed in public. The smell of newly-shed blood mingling with the stench of burnt flesh, the crashing of cymbals, and chanting, must have combined to lift the onlooker to a state of dreadful exaltation. Something of the kind, one imagines, was experienced by the audience at the Roman amphitheatre when condemned criminals fought an unequal struggle against their executioners to satisfy the citizens' blood-lust. Medieval peasantry enjoyed similar thrills as they watched bears being baited in their market places on holy days, and modern locals and tourists find some comparable emotional satisfaction in Spanish bullfights.

As the Scapegoat ceremony reached its climax, and the solitary goat was led away to be thrust over a cliff-edge to its death on the jagged rocks below, the faithful must have felt a wave of relief sweep over them; now they might enter upon another year cleansed of their accumulated guilt. Their special relationship with their god had been restored; atonement had been made and accepted.

Even those religions that have renounced animal and human sacrifices usually incorporate in their practices and belief some channel of release for the outward aggressive tendencies of their followers. For it seems to be characteristic of human nature that the more Man is required to show love towards his god and his fellow-creatures, the greater is his capacity for hatred. The one is an obverse of the other; when love is withdrawn or unrequited, the energies thus frustrated build up in the unconscious as a reservoir of aggression.

Religious ritual can tap this anti-erotic emotion and thereby relieve its corrupting pressure through the drama of sacrifice, or, where that is no longer acceptable, by focussing the believer's mind upon that legitimate target of abuse and hatred, the Devil. For in most theological systems, poised against the beneficent deity there stands his moral counterpart, representing all that is evil in creation, intent on destroying human happiness and frustrating all Man's best intentions. He is the Enemy, the projection of our worst inclinations, and the real stumbling-block between a man and his god. This adversary of every believer is there to be despised and reviled, for in exposing the Devil's evil intentions and deceitful ways through myth and exhortation, we drag into the light of day those aspects of our own nature we would most wish to conceal, and thus purge them from our overladen consciences.

To the theologian and philosopher it may suffice to express this anti-God in abstract terms, or place him within some remote cosmic hierarchy, like the Jewish Belial / Satan, with his retinue of the princes of darkness, or the Buddhist arch-tempter Mara, or the Druj ('Lie') of Zoroastrianism, with his prime agent Angra Mainyu ('Evil Mind'); or conceive of an indeterminate number of evil spirits, which, in the Christian Gnostic universe, bar the soul from penetration to the seventh heaven. To the ordinary believer, it is easier to focus the imagination upon some manifestation of evil in myth or history, like the 'Man of Lies' or 'Wicked Priest' of the Dead Sea Scrolls who opposed the Essene monks' own 'Teacher of Righteousness', or Judas Iscariot, arch-betrayer of the Lord in the Christian story, or upon groups of enemies like the Muslim Umayyads whom the Shi'a sectarians revile each year when they commemorate the martyrdom of their hero Husain on the battlefield of Karbala.

The dangers arise, of course, when such real or mythical targets of our righteous indignation become identified with living people, and this reservoir of hatred spills over, or is tapped by religious bigots or maniacal war-leaders, in fury upon our fellow-men. It is not difficult, then, to label genocidal forays as religious crusades to rid God's world of evil, and we are back to the Aztec nightmare of mass human sacrifices. There is no conflict more easily provoked or harder to control than the Holy War, the *jihad* against the infidel. Equally, on the local front, there is no readier target for our moral indignation and latent aggression than the ethnic aliens or social dissidents in our midst, whom we may accuse of undermining our religious or moral integrity.

But even for those who can resist the blandishments of the politician, religious fanatic, or their own social prejudices, the danger remains that the urge to hate may turn inwards and carry self-denial to the extreme of self-destruction. Too much introspection can over-sensitise our religious consciences and increase the load of guilt to the point where it weakens our self-confidence; we can no longer love our fellow-man, nor invite his love for us. We drive ourselves into morbid isolation and despair. Even the sacrificial act loses its efficacy as an instrument of emotional release if we substitute ourselves for the mediatory scapegoat that should carry our sin away into the wilderness; humility becomes masochism, and ascetic self-discipline vain martyrdom. On reflection, it might seem that the bloody temple-sacrifice, however gruesome and cruel it may appear at a distance, is a safer release-valve for Man's inborn aggression.

11

Religious Eroticism

The sexual associations of many religious trance-states are clear enough, particularly where the subjects are women. It is no simple literary convention that encourages the use of erotic symbolism and metaphor for the description of mystical experiences. The shaman enters into an intimate relationship with his guiding spirit; when the union is directly with the central deity, its consummation is most readily described in human sexual terms, and the bond likened to marriage. Where the god concerned is featured in myth and ritual as a young man, like Adonis, Dionysus/Apollo, or Jesus, erotic imagery is particularly apt. Thus the Christian mystics commonly draw on nuptial terminology to describe their union with the risen Lord, and, indeed, their Scriptures set the scene by referring to the Church as the 'Bride' of Christ (Revelations 22:17, etc.). Nuns are specifically bound by their vows to their Master as the 'Sacred Bridegroom', and St Teresa speaks of her ecstatic 'rapture' when she joins in communion with Christ, her 'Spouse', at the moment of experiencing the 'wound of love'. She describes how an angel appeared to her in a vision:

> In his hands I saw a long golden spear and at the end of the iron tip I seemed to see a point of fire. With this he seemed to pierce my heart several times so that it penetrated my entrails. When he drew it out I thought he was drawing them out with it and he left me completely afire with a great love of God. The pain was so sharp that it made me utter several sharp moans; and so excessive was the sweetness caused me by the intense pain that one can never wish to lose it.

Certainly there can be no doubt whence Bernini drew his inspiration for the look of transported bliss upon the saint's features in his famous sculpture.

Such erotically ecstatic experiences are not confined to the convent or mystic's retreat; in some of the less restrained fringe sects of Christianity it is not unusual for female worshippers to be stimulated by the exuberance of their chapel services to something akin to sexual orgasm.

On the whole, however, Christianity has not made overt use of sexual symbolism and practice as a medium of worship, since its philosophy, inherited from certain ascetic 'heresies' of Judaism, is generally distrustful of sex, women, and the flesh. Other Oriental faiths have cheerfully acknowledged the affinity between a religious trance-state and coital orgasm, and have not hesitated to use sex in their quest for spiritual illumination. Some, indeed, like Chinese Taoism and Indian Tantrism, have elevated sexual eroticism to the chief means of achieving religious ecstasy.

Chinese philosophy finds the polarity of male and female energies, the *yang* and *yin* respectively, the dominant principle of creation. This theme comes to have special importance in Taoism, but the idea goes far back beyond Master K'ung (*K'ung-futzu*, Confucius, sixth century, BC). The male principle, *yang*, is thought of as bright, red, pentrating, celestial, while *yin* is dull, black, receptive, abyssal; the one is identified with light, heat, and dynamism, the other with dampness, darkness, and cold. They correspond cosmically with Heaven, as the active agent of creation, and Earth, the female, passive receptacle – another reflection of the age-old concept of Mother Earth and her virile consort in the sky. From these two principles came the five elements, earth, wood, fire, metal, and water, and to the continual interplay of *yang* and *yin* is ascribed the cycle of the seasons.

Tao itself is the inexpressible source of being, the Logos, as it were, of Chinese philosophy (cf. John, ch. 1). It is the prime begetter of all creation, the mother of all things. Within this constant stream of energy, the impassive *yin* is in continual oscillation with *yang*, their energies vibrating and harmonising in a delicate balance of opposing and mutually dependent forces.

Taoist art tries to express *yang* and *yin* in a multitude of traditional symbols. Such figures as dragons, stallions, rams, horned beasts, jade, and mountains represent *yang*, the male principle, while valleys, vases, peaches, peonies, fish, and certain fungi indicate *yin*. In the combination of subjects, and the delicate pairing and fusion of colours in paintings and ceramic glazing, the principles of synthesis and harmony can be seen at work. We have a gloriously plumed Feng-bird (*yang*) flying down into a garden of peony flowers (*yin*); a dragon (*yang*) appears among swirling clouds (*yin*); and there occurs a constant representation of the Sacred Mushroom (*ling-chih*) which was believed to offer its partaker immortality.

This sexual polarity is naturally most explicit in humans, themselves microcosms of the universe. Taoism, like other Oriental philosophies, preserves and develops the primitive awareness of a unity and interdependence in creation; Man is part of the living world, an expression of that same creative force that produced the wild animals, trees, rivers, sticks, and stones, apart from which he has no separate existence. Since Tao flows through the universe, it must permeate Man, and he will achieve harmony with nature only when those inward and outward forces are in perfect accord. Taoist medicine, like its religion, centres on the means of achieving this harmony to bring patient and pietist mentally and physically into line with the pattern of energies that flow continually through his body. The special *t'ai-chi* exercises that many Chinese practise daily are designed to stimulate these inner forces, whose anatomical course is confidently mapped out and used in the art of acupuncture.

The sexual energies are also part of this central circulatory system, and a prime part of the Taoist technique for attaining self-cultivation is the full and proper use of sexual intercourse. So *yang–yin* harmony is expressed in Taoist art not only in conventional symbols gleaned from the natural world, but through very explicit representations of human love-making, illustrating the traditional six styles of sexual penetration, or the nine methods of movement and posture most favoured for mutual erotic stimulation.

Sexual intercourse plays a great part in the conservation and enhancement of the vital energies of the Taoist. Every encounter should have as its aim the giving and receiving of pleasure by each partner. By stimulating one another to the heights of sexual excitement during preliminary play and in coitus, they exchange their *yang* and *yin* energies, drawing them into their bodies through tongues, penis and vagina. In the climax of a mutual orgasm, skilled and considerate lovers can achieve a maximum concentration of *yang* and *yin*, and thus prolong their lives into a vigorous old age.

Whatever the more local origins of Indian Tantrism (seventh century, AD), it owes much to its inspiration from Taoism. Unlike classical Hinduism, Tantrism sets women on high, and even, in some teachings, on a higher plane than men. One of its sages asserts that 'Buddhahood abides in the female organ', and through sexual intercourse the adept may experience some of the god's divine nature. Through concentration on matters primarily sexual, Man's psychic centres are believed to be activated and stimulated towards an advanced degree of spiritual enlightenment. By gratifying his lust, Man helps to resolve the tension that arises in the universe through the opposition of male and female genders in creation. The sex act is therefore regarded as a channel for the highest spiritual experience, and a means of salvation. Coitus (*maithuna*) is the 'origin of all being, the root of the world, the foundation of pleasure'. Certain sects require obligatory sexual intercourse between monks and nuns. To realise the state of the

Absolute, the devotee conceives of himself as the male deity, and his partner is transfigured into a goddess, a 'field' consecrated for insemination.

In its highest stages, sexuality has a magical character. Among certain 'left-hand' sects, as the more sinister persuasions of Hinduism and Buddhism are called, intercourse with women outside the normally permitted orders, such as adulterous or incestuous relationships, are especially favoured as being more highly regarded by the divine patroness of sex, Shakti. Yet even this aberration is for the tantrik only a first step towards achieving his aim of acquiring supernatural power. He must progress by magical means to seek a union with the female demons of hell, and after that, to attract to himself the wives of the gods themselves. In a great orgy of imagined eroticism, he indulges his miraculously inflated sexual appetite in gratifying the desires of these divine beings clamouring around him for his services.

On a less elevated and mystic plane, Hinduism recognises the divine nature of mortal sex, and speaks of coitus as a sacred rite. Holy writings compare the woman to a place of worship: her hips and thighs are the sacrificial ground, her *mons veneris* the altar, her pubic hair is the sacred *kusa* grass, her moist labia the *Soma* press, her yellow vulva the fuel, and so on. The man's erected penis glows red at the glans like a firebrand, his lust is the smoke of sacrifice, orgasm is the living flame, and his semen is the oblation.

The walls of Hindu temples are commonly adorned with erotic sculptures, portraying the gods and goddesses in various coital positions. Bestiality also has its part to play in heavenly sex, and is well represented in the Black Pagoda at Konarak (thirteenth century AD), and some of the temples at Bhubaneswar (*c.* 1000 AD). One myth has Shiva create the animal world through his copulation with prototypal females of each species. He begat the Maruts through fertilising the goddess Prithivi when she had taken the form of a cow. He enjoyed intercourse with Parvati 'in the elephant mode', and from this happy congress was born Ganesa, the god of good fortune.

It was thought that animal sex was more voluptuous than human, and one of the prizes open to adepts in various yogic disciplines was the ability to assume animal form at will in order to copulate with beasts. Failing such magical metamorphosis, actual bestiality by humans of either sex was not uncommon. It was said that the Malla princess Mallika, wife of Prasenajit of Kosala (sixth century BC), gratified her lust with a pet dog, while her husband sought satisfaction with a she-goat. Later, pet dogs and monkeys were sometimes trained for use in harems. In erotic manuals, male and female sexual types are classified in animal terms such as hare, buck, horse, and elephant, and postures appropriate to these animals are recommended for sexual intercourse, each position to be accompanied by the corresponding noise.

It has been suggested that bestiality may be a relic of old fertility rites practised by Indian tribal peoples with their domestic animals or beasts of the chase, to ensure the fecundity of the earth and its creatures. One is reminded of the figures dressed in animal skins portrayed on the walls of palaeolithic caves in Europe; were they similarly identifying themselves with the beasts their hunters sought in the world outside, and indulging in some real or simulated bestial rites to encourage the abundance of game and the success of the chase?

It is frequently pointed out in Hindu religious texts that sexual union has its dangers, since to expend one's semen is to lose some vital force and thus deplete a man's reserves of spiritual advantage. If he can retain this precious liquid within his body, he is able to accumulate great power for himself. Semen is reckoned the quintessence of all manifested things. It exists in a subtle form throughout a man's body. When he begins sexual congress, this force is withdrawn and concentrated in his genitals in preparation for emission at climax. But actual ejaculation must result in spiritual loss, whereas its retention builds up a kind of magical attraction which will make a man irresistible to others.

The most obvious method of semen retention is, of course, to avoid sex altogether and remain in a state of absolute continence. To resist all sexual temptations is to subjugate the senses, a conquest of the 'lower' self by the 'higher', the desired goal of Jains and Buddhists. Hindu legend tells of sages of old who achieved so much power by their celibacy that they provoked the envy of the gods, who sent beautiful nymphs to parade their charms before the righteous men when their power was at its peak, with the intention of seducing them into involuntary ejaculation of their semen.

One of Shiva's aspects is that of the ascetic, and representations show him carrying an unstrung bow, symbol of his passivity. Similarly, the Jain meditative pose called *nich-medra* ('down-penis') has the adept standing quite relaxed, arms hanging down by his side but not touching his body, and his mind 'free from sexual thoughts, with penis pendant'.

Tantrik teachings, while strenuously advocating the importance of sexual intercourse for spiritual ends, nevertheless continually stress the need for controlling seminal emission and absorbing the fluid into the adept's own body: 'The plough (penis) and the bulls (testes) the wise old man will use for ploughing his own land and sowing his own seed, so that he can eat his own fruit.' This last phrase, 'eating one's own fruit', is variously interpreted: the more gross reading is that the yogi shall stimulate his penis orally when in certain postures and, on ejaculation, swallow his semen.

A more frenzied method of preserving vital energies is deliberately to excite one's sexual desires by every kind of erotic stimulation and then, through various yogic techniques, withhold actual emission, or so contrive one's *vega* ('jerk'), or ejaculation, that the semen remains within the body. The discipline of self-control required for these rites is of a high order, and is reckoned to achieve great spiritual bliss.

The adept must prepare himself with periods of intense concentration on sex and the genital organs. In one form of meditative technique, the ascetic focuses his thoughts on Kama, the god of lust, and keeps his eyes steadfastly fixed upon the tip of his erect penis, or on a woman's vulva. This is intended to draw down the sexual powers of the deity.

In *stripuja* ('woman-worship'), a group of devotees gather for worship and concentrated meditation, with a nude woman, or more particularly, her genitals, as the prime focus of attention. She is especially selected by the guru in charge, given instruction, and consecrated for her role as an incarnation of the goddess Shakti. The men taking part prepare themselves for five days beforehand by eating spiced food and taking drugs, alcohol, and other supposed aphrodisiacs. They must also refrain from all sexual intercourse during this time. Then they come together for the meditative ritual and ceremonial feast.

The incarnate goddess is first brought before the company, sprinkled with wine, and ritually sanctified for adoration by her devotees. The worship takes various forms, and one of them was thus described by an observer writing at the beginning of this century:

> The woman is seated on an altar with legs spread wide apart to display the sacred symbol, the *yoni* [vulva], which the priest kisses and to which he offers food and libations in sacred vessels called *argha*, which are shaped like the *yoni*. After these offerings have been consecrated by touching them to the living *yoni*, they are distributed among the worshippers and eaten. (O. A. Wall, *Sex and Sex Worship*, London, 1909, p. 480.)

The woman thus honoured is not necessarily selected for her youth, beauty, or virtue. Often she will be repulsively ugly and ill-formed, or chosen for her low caste or depraved and debauched character. The idea is to concentrate the attention of the worshippers on the vulva itself as the prime embodiment of the female sex principle, to the exclusion of all considerations of beauty, birth, and breeding.

After the worship feasting may commence, the men being served by women wearing nothing but bells around their hips and ankles, which are reckoned to excite the divine and erotic passions of the participants. The ritual meal lasts for hours until each adept has been aroused to a state of great sexual tension, which he must keep under strict control. If he can refrain from ejaculation he will be reckoned to have diverted his sexual energies from the physical to the psychic plane, and to have thereby achieved a high degree of spiritual exaltation.

Other, more testing rites are practised in private. In one of these, the objects of the tantrik's adoration is a young virgin, just growing into womanhood. She comes to live with him for some weeks, and he waits upon her like a servant, bathing and dressing her, and generally attending to her needs. At first he will merely sleep in the same room with her, but later, in growing degrees of intimacy, he will lie at her feet, then by her side through the night, and finally hold her in close embrace. But at no time will he allow himself to have full intercourse with the object of his attentions.

In those practices where sexual intercourse is allowed to culminate in ejaculation, other means of 'eating one's own fruit' are recommended. These involve a reabsorption of the semen through a combination of respiratory and muscular actions at the moment of emission. One technique is known as *urdhva-retas* ('upward-flow'), in fact a kind of *coitus reservatus.* During the climax of the man's sex act the semen is said to be converted into a vital force and given an 'upward flow'. More prosaically, Western doctors describe it as a pressure upon the urethra and contraction of the anus, combined with certain breathing restrictions at the time of ejaculation, which results in the semen being discharged into the bladder, to be voided later in the urine.

But whatever the physical explanation of the exercise, this internal seminal ejaculation is said to prolong the climactic moment into a sustained sensation of indescribable ecstasy. The intense orgiastic excitement is diverted from the physiological to the psychological plane, and then to the realms of spiritual awareness, bringing the adept to the highest state of blissful enlightenment:

> The pairing couple, during this act of esoteric *maithuna*, represent the union of the genders, and embody a plane of being where thought is still, the breath immobilised, and semen arrested, and where man is able to contemplate the ultimate reality face to face. The supreme bliss that proceeds from ritual sexuality is believed to be the height of religious experience. In this state of non-duality all differences vanish, and everything, high and low, good and bad, ugly and beautiful, is held to be the same. It is while in this pose that the couple apprehend the mystery of the whole cosmic process and taste the transcendent bliss of divine experience. (Walker, *Hindu World*, ii, p. 393.)

Such frustrated or perverted sexual practices can bring about abnormal physiological states of brain excitement leading to trance phenomena, including heightened suggestibility and delusions of 'possession'; the same is also true of more normal sexual gratification if sufficiently prolonged or repeated. A feature of the late Aleister Crowley's psychic experiments was the inducement of trance states in his subjects by excessive sexual exertions. He dignified the technique with the name 'Erotocomatose Lucidity', and it seems to have owed much to tantrik practice:

> The candidate is made ready for the ordeal by general athletic training and fasting. On the appointed day he is attended by one or more experienced attendants whose duty is to exhaust him sexually by every known means. The candidate will sink into a sleep of utter exhaustion but he must be again sexually stimulated and then again allowed to fall asleep. This alternation is to continue indefinitely until the candidate is in a state which

is neither sleep nor waking, and in which his spirit is set free by perfect exhaustion of the body . . . communes with the most Highest and the Most Holy Lord God of its Being, Maker of Heaven and Earth. (Quoted by W. Sargant. *The Mind Possessed*, London, 1973, p. 94f.)

Crowley's circle of fellow-occultists believed not only that they could attain spiritual enlightenment through sexual means, but that they could influence material objects by the magical power they generated. They claimed that success in almost any magical operation, from the invocation of the god to procuring a great treasure, could be achieved by the application of the appropriate sexual technique. Thus, to invoke the powers of a god into themselves they mentally concentrated on the deity throughout their sexual intercourse, building up the divine form in their imaginations and attempting to imbue it with life. At the moment of orgasm they identified themselves with the god, mentally envisaging their own bodies and that of the manifested deity as one. 'By the right use of this secret,' records Crowley in his diaries, 'man may impose his will on Nature Herself . . . though all recorded knowledge is destroyed, it would be possible for an adept of this secret to restore it'.

While the Hindu writings dwell a good deal on the perverse and unlikely aspects of sex, they also have much to say about normal sexual relationships that is both acute and sensitive. It is recognised that female sexual feelings are very different from those of the male, and that, like a eunuch incapable of ever knowing sexual gratification, a man is utterly unable to understand the female orgasm, or a woman a man's ejaculative climax. Masculine pleasure centres on the actual penetration of the woman with his penis and in the subsequent spermal emission, but a woman derives equal satisfaction from the assurance that she is desired by her partner and capable of pleasing him. She responds to the man's advances with her mind and the whole of her body so that, at its deepest, her climax is much more complete and fulfilling than a man's.

There is a Greek legend that tells of the seer Teiresias being chosen by Zeus and Hera to pronounce upon the question of whether a man or woman derives most pleasure from sexual intercourse. He replied that of the ten parts of coitus, a man enjoys one only; but a woman's senses revel in all ten to the full. The Hindu traditions have a story with a similar import about a royal sage named Bhangasvana who had the misfortune to incur the wrath of the god Indra. Being without male issue, the king recklessly performed a sacrifice to Indra's rival, Agni, the fire god. It proved successful, since the king thereupon begot a hundred sons. However, Indra took his revenge by leading the monarch one day to a magical lake. When he plunged in to refresh himself, he found to his horror that he had been changed into a woman.

Overcome with shame, the king returned to the palace and confessed his change of sex to his courtiers. He handed over control of the kingdom to his sons and retired into the forest and there lived as the wife of a hermit. No less fruitful, he bore the man a further hundred sons. When they were old enough, Bhangasvana sent them to the palace to rule the kingdom jointly with his first hundred sons.

However, Indra, his wrath still unabated, heard of this development and sent a messenger to stir up strife between the two sets of princes. Learning of this quarrel, the poor sage could only weep and bemoan his fate. At length Indra appeared to him in person and disclosed the reason for his awful predicament. The sage begged forgiveness, and Indra relented, but asked Bhangasvana to choose whether he would sooner have the first hundred sons remain alive or the second, and whether for the future he would prefer to return to his original sex or remain as a woman. To the first proposition, Bhangasvana replied that he would wish to preserve the sons he had borne as a woman, since the fruit of his own body meant more to him than those children he had merely sired. To the second question he replied that he would wish to continue as a woman since in that capacity he enjoyed his sex life so much more.

The sage's answer is said to have pleased the god, and it certainly makes a significant comment on female sensibilities. Not only can intercourse be a more deeply satisfying experience for a woman truly in love with her partner than it can for a man, but she is biologically conditioned to bear far greater responsibility for the rearing of any resulting offspring. Fathers everywhere never cease to be amazed at the almost supernatural perception a mother possesses in her understanding of her baby and its needs; it is the mother who awakes at the first whimper from the cot, when most men would be happy to sleep on undisturbed. Without that deep affinity between mother and child, the comparatively immature human infant could not possibly survive the first hazardous years of existence outside the womb.

No matter how vociferously our feminists may claim equality between the sexes and freedom of choice in all matters, the basic differences in sexual attitudes cannot be disguised and are of far greater significance than any cultural or economic pressures. A satisfying relationship for a woman means far more than the sex act, which biologically is no more than a prelude to motherhood. Her more profound physical involvement in coitus and its greater sensual rewards are in proportion to her deeper commitment to the child that may be conceived.

Again, it is the female who initiates the mating procedure by sexual display , whether, in a non-human oestral situation, by exhibiting some bright distinguishing signal of her readiness for copulation, such as the pink swelling around a female chimpanzee's genitals, or, in the human species, by attracting attention to herself through donning provocative or exotic dress at social events.

From the moment she conceives, the female has prime

responsibility for the generative process, and at its culmination at the child-bed there is little place for the man. Most primitive societies would look aghast at the reputedly growing practice in the western world of having the husband present at the child's birth. Parturition, and everything pertaining to it, is one of the deepest, and possibly most biologically-motivated of all human taboos.

This profound involvement by the woman in sex and generation is reflected in her greater susceptibility to certain religious emotions. Not unnaturally, it is she who has always taken an active role in the worship of the Earth-mother, and particularly as we shall see in the next chapter, in the ritual lamentation for the dead fertility god. This very widespread custom has its basis in the myth portraying the death of the vegetation deity at the hands of his enemies, the heat and drought of summer. He descends into the underworld for regeneration, and, in due season with the awakening of Spring, he emerges again, resurrected to new life.

The ritual of 'lamentation' is essentially a sexual exercise by which, in prayer, song, and drama, the god's female devotees persuade him to demonstrate his virility and bring new life to the barren soil. They urge him to come forth from the nether regions as the forerunner of spring herbage, enticing him as a snake-charmer drawing a snake from its hole, or as a woman will conjure her lover's penis to erection. The symbolic object of the 'mourners'' attention was often a bed or pot of shallowly-planted seedlings which had the property of germinating quickly under the heat of the sun, and as rapidly dying away again before the end of the day. These 'gardens' were named after the god Adonis, or Tammuz, and we have a passing reference to the cult in the prophet Ezekiel's vision of the Jerusalem Temple:

> Then he brought me to the entrance of the north gate of the house of Yahweh; and behold, there sat women bewailing Tammuz. Then he said to me, Have you seen this, O son of man? You will see greater abominations than these . . . (8: 14f.)

Exactly what the 'abominations' performed by the women before their sleeping god were we cannot be sure, although we may guess that they involved some form of sexual display to entice the young shoots above ground. In this capacity the women were acting out their role of 'sacred prostitutes', that very special class of devotees essential to the fertility religions, whose task was to use their sexuality to stimulate by one means or the other the renewal of the agricultural year. If we may identify the original 'Adonis' vegetation with the Sacred Mushroom, well-known for its almost magical appearance and as speedy withering away, we have a clue to the nature of its 'lamenters' ' activities. There is a tradition recorded for us by Josephus that, in order to capture the Mandrake and stop it 'shrinking away from the touch', it was necessary to pour over it a woman's urine and menstrual blood (*War*, VII, 181). Doubtless the cult prostitute achieved this directly, by exposing her genitals to that part of the ground where the fungus was thought to lie dormant.

Self-exposure of menstruants for vegetative purposes is elsewhere mentioned in ancient writings. Pliny, the natural historian, tells us that in order to utilise the harmful effect of menses on 'caterpillars, worms, beetles, and other vermin', menstruating women walked around the cornfields naked, and the vermin fell to the ground. It was said that the pesticidal qualities of this powerful substance were first discovered in Cappadocia, 'owing to a plague there of Spanish fly . . . women walk through the middle of the fields with their clothes pulled above their buttocks' (*Natural History*, XXVIII, 78).

Quite apart from the menstrual aspect of the Mandrake's cultic appropriation, the mere presence of the prostitutes would have been reckoned a powerful influence upon the phallic-shaped herb. The ability of a woman to induce an erection in a man, apparently without any control on the part of the man himself, or even the necessity for her physical contact with the organ, was a great source of wonder to the ancients. It was reckoned to be sorcery, and as such viewed with apprehension and some fear by men, not unmixed with religious awe. This was particularly the case with those mystic orders that made use of the sexual powers of women for their secret rites. Where, indeed, we find strong, even fanatical misogyny displayed in sectarian attitudes, such as in certain persuasions of early Judaism and later Hinduism, we may suspect some involvement in sex rites either in their past or in current esoteric practice. The readiness of the medieval Church to hound supposed witches in their midst, betrayed deep-rooted antagonisms towards the female sex which possibly reveal more about Christianity's own history than the culpability of the poor wretches its leaders had burnt at the stake (see Chapter Fourteen).

The telepathic control believed to have been exercised by such females, known the world over as the 'evil eye', came originally from this ability to arouse men's passions. The Latin *fascinus,* from which our 'fascination' comes, meant not only 'bewitching', but was the proper name for a god whose emblem was an erect penis, and is related to the Greek word for 'sorcerer', *baskanos*. It was believed that the malign influences of 'fascination', which came to be extended to any form of mental domination, could be averted – on the principle of like repelling like – by wearing on the person a replica of a phallus, rather as the Christian symbol of the Cross, also a fertility symbol in origin, is freely displayed to ward off evil.

Whatever the magical rites performed by the devotees of Adonis, their actions were accompanied by loud screeching and wailing which were apparently intended to have some erotic effect, to judge from the sexual associations of the lamentation vocabulary. There is an interesting parallel here in the hysterical weeping and screaming of young female pop fans in the presence of their guitar-jerking idols on the stage.

Screaming is just another form of emotional release, but there is no reason to doubt that the grief expressed by those cultic mourners for their dead god was real enough, and the tears they shed were as genuine as those we see streaming from the eyes of pious women every Good Friday as they contemplate the crucifixion of their Lord. Equally, the female votaries of the goddess Ishtar, the consort of the dead Tammuz, would have identified themselves with the suffering mother as she sought in vain for his broken body in the underworld, quite as sincerely as those Catholic women who grieve with the broken-hearted Virgin at the foot of the Cross. And there can be few female admirers of Michelangelo's masterpiece who can stand unmoved emotionally before the Pietà, however much their more critical faculties may doubt the probability of the events it commemorates.

The essential factor in these lamentation rituals has always been that they should provide an outlet for repressed emotions; it is not the degree of historicity accorded the events remembered that measures the effectiveness of the spiritual exercise, but the sympathy the participants can bring to the object of their worship. The whole purpose of religious mythology is not to convey historical facts, as some of our pedantic commentators would have us believe, but to present in dramatic form some facet of human experience that will evoke a response in our subconscious and open the floodgates to our repressed emotions.

There is in human beings, and in women in particular, a capacity for sympathetic grief which demands dramatic expression, however artificially contrived the events and persons portrayed. As Aristotle said of tragedy some twenty-two centuries ago, it is 'the imitation of an action that is serious, and also, as having magnitude, complete in itself . . . with incidents arousing pity and terror, with which to accomplish its purgations of these emotions' (*Poetics*, 6).

The female faculty for altruistic suffering matches her

capacity for sexual fulfilment. The curse upon womenkind pronounced in Eden has the ring of profound psychological truth: 'I will greatly multiply your pain in child-bearing; in pain you shall bring forth children, yet your (sexual) desire shall be to your man even while he rules over you' (Genesis 3:16).

12

The Earth-Mother

To judge from some of the earliest of Man's archaeological artifacts and mythologies, a very primitive concept of the deity was female, expressing the idea of sexual receptiveness and maternity in the natural world. From Western Asia, the South Russian plain, and the valley of the Don, have come female figurines known, somewhat optimistically, as 'Venuses'. They depict women whose large pendulous breasts and hugely distended bellies emphasise the characteristics of womanhood and pregnancy. 'Venus'-figures in bone, ivory, stone, and basrelief, were introduced into Eastern and Central Europe at the beginning of the Upper Palaeolithic period (Old Stone Age) around 40–30,000 years ago, by an Asiatic migration, as part of what is known as the Gravettian culture (from the blade-tool, or gravette, that characterises its technology). Its diffusion-centre was Western Asia and the Eurasiatic steppes and it came through the loess-lands of the Danube to Moravia and Austria. In the most famous of these 'Venus'-figurines, from Willendorf near Vienna, the face is featureless and the arms are hardly represented but, as elsewhere, the breasts, abdomen, and buttocks are grossly exaggerated, and there are traces of red ochre still visible in the pores of the limestone, indicating an attempt to symbolise blood, the essence of life.

In a rock-shelter at Laussel in the valley of the Beune, near Les Eyzies in the Dordogne, an almost equally well-known carving was found, showing a woman, apparently pregnant, holding in her right hand a bison's horn. Again the body had been coloured with red pigment to denote life-blood. On the ground were found four other similar reliefs, two of which were of women holding horns, one was of a male figure apparently in the act of shooting with a bow and arrow (presuming that such weapons were in use in Palaeolithic times), and the fourth has been variously interpreted as either a woman giving birth, or one engaging in sexual intercourse with a man lying between her legs.

Whether such representations were meant to be identified with one particular divinity is open to question, but they certainly do indicate a lively interest in the principle of natural fecundity. Later, in the succeeding Chalcolithic (Bronze–Stone) period and Bronze Age, the cult of the mother-goddess was diffused from this same Eurasian cradleland, and her adoration became a predominant feature of religious culture from India to Britain. For, between the fifth and third millennia BC the emblems and inscriptions of the cult became firmly established in the Fertile Crescent, in Western Asia, the Indus Valley, the Aegean, and Crete, and it was destined to play a vital role in the subsequent development of all those cultures that developed from, or were influenced by the religions of the Ancient Near East, including Christianity.

At the heart of the cult of the Mother-goddess lies the powerful conception of the earth as a mighty womb in which all life is engendered. Beneath the surface are eternal fires that quicken gestation, and which every now and then betray their presence in erupting volcanoes, and in hot springs and geysers fed from underground cauldrons. Here is no abstract theological concept, but an observable phenomenon of nature. It speaks to a man's deepest sensibilities, his biological and emotional relationship with his mother and his wife.

But if we speak of origins, it were better to understand our 'man' generically: it is perhaps to women that we should more fittingly credit this vital concept of the Earth-mother. It is significant that the earliest figurines are not, like so much later religious iconography, of mother and child, or of a warrior-king as god. These belong to a time where the male deity had usurped the Goddess's prime place in the pantheon, and her function had become merely that of the god's mother, or his consort. A man may appreciate the Earth-mother's contribution to the fruitfulness of nature, and cast himself upon her mercy as the source of those necessities that determine his survival; but it is the woman who can more fully enter into an emotional relationship with her Goddess. She can feel with her divine mistress the quickening of life in the womb, and when she is herself in travail, she will call instinctively for help and comfort to the Universal Mother. In the words of an eminent woman anthropologist:

> The knowledge that there was a living entity within her, coming without her knowledge and from whence she could not tell as a gift from an unseen power, must have brought with it that feeling of protection, which after the birth will culminate in that passionate love which will cause a mother to sacrifice her own life in defence of her offspring. These are physical sensations and mental agonies of which the man is entirely ignorant, but to the woman they are indications of a mysterious power, unseen but overruling. (Margaret Murray, *The Genesis of Religion*, London, 1963, p. 69.)

Sexual attraction has always presented mankind with its deepest mystery, but even when the man's role in the generative process was eventually recognised, it must have seemed almost ridiculously trivial when compared with the woman's part in creating life. She not only formed the baby with her blood, but after nine months of tender care urged it forth through an impossibly narrow orifice, and then fed it for many months afterwards from the secretions of her own body. Even the initiative in activating the male organ to perform its brief function lay with the woman; she could charm it to erection through her own dark powers of erotic suggestion, and by her wiles tempt her partner from more manly pursuits in the hunting-field to seek her soft embrace and implant his seed within her womb. Long after his excitement had subsided and he had turned away to sleep or sulk in post-coital lethargy, the warmth of his embrace would linger in the woman's breast, the germ she had so skilfully extracted from his loins would curdle the blood in her body to begin the process of making new life. For long months she would cherish within her that precious creature, flesh of her flesh, blood of her blood, until at length she could bring it forth to perpetuate her line in successive generations.

Small wonder that the earliest political systems were probably matriarchal: the queen-mother was the progenitress of the clan, while her consort played a junior role in government. She might choose an annual lover from among her entourage, but not uncommonly his term of office ended with his being sacrificed to the gods to ensure that the fertility of the land would continue during the following year.

With the establishment of husbandry and the domestication of flocks and herds, the physiological facts of paternity would have been more clearly appreciated and given due weight in religious symbolism. As the male sperm was implanted in the female to produce young, so it was thought that the rain that 'impregnated' Mother Earth must equally derive from a heavenly 'Father', ejaculating his seed in a mighty orgasm. In the sacred writings of India we find the furrow thought of as a 'vulva' (*yoni*), and the seeds in the earth as 'semen' (see *Satapatha Brahmana* VII 2,2,5). Similarly, in Anglo-Saxon England, the same symbolism exists in an old charm to make the land fertile, probably based on an earlier, half-remembered religious tradition:

> Erce, Erce, Erce, Earth Mother,
> may the Almighty Eternal Lord
> grant you fields to increase and flourish,
> fields fruitful and healthy,
> shining harvests of shafts of millet,
> broad harvests of barley . . .

Hail to thee, Earth, Mother of Men;
Bring forth now in God's embrace,
filled with good for the use of man.

(See H. R. Ellis Davidson, *Gods and Myths of Northern Europe*, Harmondsworth, 1964, p. 114.)

This evocative concept of earth and heaven joined in wedlock gave rise to myths and rituals concerned with a 'sacred marriage' between the Sky-father and the Earth-mother. The Greek dramatist Aeschylus (sixth to fifth century BC) has Aphrodite say in a fragment of *Danaides*:

The pure Sky yearns passionately to pierce the Earth,
And yearns likewise for her marriage.
Rain falls from the bridegroom Sky, impregnating the Earth,
And she brings forth her brood for mortal men –
Pastures of flocks and corn, Demeter's gift,
While trees from that same watery brilliance grow
Their fruits to fulness.

(*Tragg. Graec. Frag.* (Nauck), 44)

The fertilising rain was borne by the wind, the 'breath' of the god, personified among the Aztecs of Mexico as Quetzalcoatl. Legend has it that when his time of power was well advanced, the fertility goddess Coatlicue, mistress of the earth, mother of life, death, and the gods, stripped herself naked and sat exposing her beautiful opened vulva before him to tempt him to impregnate her expectant womb. One myth recounts that, at a festival, the goddess offered the god-king a bowl of alcoholic pulque prepared from the agave heart. Then, as he became intoxicated, she gave him sacred mushrooms and induced a trance-like ecstasy in which he abandoned his austerity and ravished her.

Sometimes the male deity is identified with the sun, as the prime fertiliser of the earth. But even in such a cosmology, it is the moon who rules the heavens, her cycle of twenty-eight days reflecting the menstrual period of her patroness, the Great Mother. As Pliny says:

the moon is rightly believed to be the star of the spirit . . . that saturates the earth and fills bodies by its approach and empties them by its departure . . . the blood even of humans increases and diminishes with its light, and leaves and herbage . . . are sensitive to it, the same force penetrating into all things. (*Natural History*, II, 221.)

He warns, furthermore, that menstrual discharge that occurs when the moon is not visible is particularly dangerous:

if this female force should issue when the moon or the sun is in eclipse, it will cause irremediable harm; no less so when there is no moon. At such seasons sexual intercourse brings death and disease upon a man. (II, 78.)

In myth, the Queen-goddess's consort is portrayed as a husband or son, symbolising short-lived vegetation appearing in the spring and doomed to die in the summer heat and remain dormant during the winter. In due season he must be revived with sacrifices, lamentation, and erotic ritual, as we saw earlier in the last chapter, all designed to stir the sluggish energies of nature to fresh creative activity.

In ancient Mesopotamia, it is the Sumerian Dumuzi, the Akkadian Tammuz, who is reunited with the fertility goddess Inanna, the Semitic Ishtar, in the spring. He is pictured as a youthful, suffering god who, as a symbol of natural growth, is doomed to die annually in the normal rotation of the seasons, and who must pass into the land of darkness. From this underworld he has to be rescued by his loving spouse/mother at the turn of the year.

In the re-creative ritual commemorating the return of life to the upper world, the part of the 'dead' god *redivivus* was enacted by the local rulers who were joined in a 'sacred marriage' ceremony with their queens or cult-priestesses assuming the role of the Mother-goddess. A hymn to Ishtar written for the cult of the deified king Isin-Dagan (2258–2237 BC) commemorates his 'marriage' as Tammuz with the goddess, at the season of her return with her consort from the land of the dead. Images of the king and his divine mistress show them lying side-by-side on a marble bed in the sanctuary. When the union had been consummated, the king acquired the status of the dying-and-rising god, symbol of life and death. But, significantly, throughout the hymn it is the goddess who takes the initiative: it is to her 'far-famed temple' that the king went, bringing her offerings of cakes 'to set the table for the feast', and it is she who embraced her beloved husband, while he gladly accepted the favours she graciously bestowed upon him.

The Babylonian spring-festival of *Akitu* was marked by the ceremonial abdication of the ruling king and his reinstallation in the shrine of Marduk. This deity had replaced the fertility god Tammuz on the change of the land's capital to Babylon, but he preserved many of the functions and characteristics of the divine son/consort of Ishtar. On the eleventh of the month of Nisan, a 'marriage' was solemnised between the king, now freshly invigorated by his reinstatement as the incarnation of the god's creative power, and a priestess, probably of royal blood. For the occasion a bridal bower was erected on one of the stages of the stepped *ziggurat,* the sacred 'mountain' of the Mesopotamian sanctuaries, and decorated with spring foliage. There the union was consummated, symbolising the fertilisation of the earth by the god, and the encouragement of animal and human fecundity. But again, it is the priestess who ritually summons the king to her sacred embrace on the connubial couch and who, as representing the goddess, bestows on him through their intercourse a divine but subservient status in the creative process.

From the Near East, the cult of the Mother-goddess passed before 3000 BC through Anatolia to the Aegean and the Eastern Mediterranean, bearing with it its full regalia of cult objects, the dove, snake, double-axe, horns of consecration, phalli, and the female figurines we noted earlier. In the goddess's representations she is everywhere accompanied by sacred pillars, trees, and mountains, and has a retinue of wild beasts and horned sacrificial victims.

In Crete, home of the first civilized Europeans and centre of the brilliant Minoan culture, the Mother-goddess cult held sway from about the middle of the fourth millenium. By then, connections with Asia Minor had been established, and when, by the Middle Minoan period (2100–1700 BC), this relationship had become intensified, the Goddess emerged as an individualised, anthropomorphic figure embracing the functions of Earth-mother, Mountain-goddess, Mistress of Trees, Lady of Wild Beasts, and Guardian of the Dead. When her cult passed to mainland Greece, these various aspects and attributes became divided among a number of different goddesses, but in Crete she was essentially *the* Goddess, *par excellence*, Britomartis or Diktyanna, later identified with Artemis and her other Greek associates.

The double-axe, which is such a prominent feature of the Asiatic and Cretan Mother-goddess cult, is a clear fertility symbol with sexual associations. The lower edges of the blade represent the woman's opened thighs, the central shaft-hole her vagina, and the shaft itself the inserted penis. The expressive graphic symbolism finds philological support in the words for the implement in ancient Sumerian, Indo-European, and Semitic.

The snake symbolism, which is also one of the most powerfully evocative aspects of the Goddess's cult, is again clearly sexual. The darting, thrusting reptile has obvious phallic associations, and its emergence from holes in the ground is especially significant for a vegetation cult. But there is more to snake symbolism than its fertility associations. The serpent who introduced our legendary forebears in the Garden of Eden to the delights of sex, was the embodiment of the Devil, and it is no accident that the snake heads the list of children's 'hates'.

There seems to be an inborn aversion to snake-forms in our species which is paralleled by similar instinctive reactions among our closest living relatives the chimpanzees, gorillas, and orang utans. These animals also exhibit great fear of snakes from the time they leave the security of their mother's side to explore the treacherous world about them. For them such an aversion-response has an important survival value, and we seem to have inherited it from our primate ancestors.

The snake, then, in religious symbolism expresses our own ambivalent attitude to sex, finding it at once fascinating and compulsive, and yet frightening in its powers to dominate our will. Sex can be a means of demonstrating a sublime love and beauty in human relationships, and yet, uncontrolled, it can drive Man irresistibly towards a self-destructive possessiveness. This duality is fully expressed in the worship of the Mother-goddess, as we shall see: she is hated as well as loved, inspiring abject terror in her subjects as well as utter devotion. She is the dark and terrible Kali of India, as well as the glamorous and voluptuous Greek Aphrodite.

It must seem to us somewhat incongruous that the Mother-goddess should be credited in so much of her mythology with being a 'virgin', like the Canaanite battle-goddess Anat, sister-consort of Baal, or the classical Artemis, patroness of all wildlife and of women in child-birth. We should, however, appreciate that 'virginity' in this context is not indicative of having an intact hymen, but has to be understood in terms of the old fertility philosophy, which maintained that the first-born of the womb was the best of all a female's progeny because it was formed from her menstrual blood when it was at its most powerful. Similarly, next in excellence to the first-born of a young woman, a 'virgin' in this sense, was the child of an older female conceiving for the first time, just prior to menopause.

The idea seems to have been that, for some reason, irregular menstrual discharge was considered more powerful than that which occurred at normal monthly intervals. An adolescent girl's first period, like that of the older woman who had retained her virginity into later life, was reckoned 'spontaneous', and thus all-powerful. 'It is strong enough,' says the ever-credulous Pliny, 'to make mares miscarry even at the sight of it over long distances' (*Natural History*, XXVIII, 79).

In biblical mythology this idea of the potency of the first and last menses inspires stories of heroes being born to aged, previously barren women, like Isaac (Genesis, ch. 17), Samuel (I Samuel 1), and John the Baptist (Luke 1:18), or, in the case of Jesus, to a virgin (Luke 1:27).

As the first-born of human progeny was considered the most favoured, so the first-born of animals and the first-reaped fruits of harvest were reckoned as the prime produce, and alone worthy of sacrifice to the deity (cf. Exodus 22:29). As might be expected, so potent an offspring of Mother-earth as the Mandrake-mushroom was believed to have been conceived of the Goddess's most powerful 'menses', a worthy product of her 'virginity'. The *Amanita muscaria,* or Fly-agaric, is a denizen of the conifer forests, which habitat has given the Sacred Mushroom so much of its mythology and, incidentally, localises the possible origin of the cult to a coniferous area. The ancients believed that it was the resin from such trees that nourished the fungus (see Pliny, *op. cit.*, XII, 96), and spoke of that mysteriously powerful substance that provided fuel for processional torches as well as an aromatic ingredient for incense, as the tree's 'menses'. The ancient botanist Theophrastus (fourth to third century BC) says that the resinous extraction of the Silver-fir was the 'menses of Eileithyia', goddess of child-birth, whose symbols included, appropriately enough, the ceremonial resin-torch. The writer adds that 'the prophets' are required to make atonement to the goddess for the extraction of the tree's 'menstrual blood'.

An ancient Akkadian incantation, probably directed to the Sacred Mushroom, also refers to its coniferous source:

'O *kukru, kukru, kukru*, in the pure, holy mountains thou hast engendered Little-ones by a sacred prostitute, Seeds-of-a-pine by a temple harlot. . . .' (*Maqglu*, VI, 37–40.)

with the plea that whatever sorcery may have been thus begotten shall be dispersed.

If the Earth-mother's menses were thought to exude through the bark of her arboreal offspring, the cedar, an even more direct and powerful source of this creative substance could be seen in the bitumen or pitch that appeared in various places on the earth's surface. In particular, the lumps of bitumen that floated periodically on the waters of the Dead Sea in Palestine, the Asphalt Lake, as it was known to the Romans, were believed to come straight from the womb of the Earth-mother. The floor of the Rift Valley in which the Sea is situated, plunges far beneath the level of the surrounding terrain, indeed it lies some thirteen hundred feet below normal sea-level. Its profundity must therefore have been quite evident to observers from the earliest times, and they would have recognised that here the earth's surface came closer than anywhere else to the womb of the Mother-goddess. It followed, therefore, that the lumps of sticky bitumen they saw on the Sea's waters must come directly from the terrestrial matrix, and tradition has it that the precious substance was considered of particular value in the treatment of gynaecological disorders in women (Dioscorides [first century AD], *De Materia Medica* I 73). It was, however, difficult to collect, and Josephus records that the only way boatmen could detach their 'tenacious and glutinous' cargo from the boat's hold, once having hauled the lumps aboard, was by loosening it with 'the menstrual discharge of women' (*War*, IV, 479f.), on the principle of like repelling like.

The supposed proximity of the Dead Sea valley to the centre of the earth's womb received further support in the hot springs that favoured a place called Callirrhoe, on the east side of the Asphalt Lake. As late as the last century it was popularly believed that the hot water, once utilised by King Herod's physicians to relieve his mortal pains, was released from the lower regions by evil spirits, to ensure that it was not available in hell to assuage the suffering of the damned. Another legend has it that King Solomon, on hearing about the thinness of the earth's crust at this point, sent a messenger to open the springs for the royal use. However, before the unfortunate envoy departed on his way, the king judiciously took the precaution of having the man's eardrums pierced so that he should not be deterred from his task by hearing the awful threats uttered by the demons in hell.

The female principle, then, was considered pre-eminent in the natural order. The Goddess's consort was at first a secondary figure, reflecting the male's subordinate role in the creative process. Later he came to play a more dominant part in society and religious faith and practice, and in India we can see the coalescence of these two traditions.

In the north-west an earlier Mother-goddess cult was already firmly established when the tall, light-skinned Aryan-speaking intruders from the Eurasian plains of Southern Russia arrived in the Sind and Punjab between 1500 BC and 1200 BC. They had made their way across the Caucasus Mountains and the Iranian plateau, through Transoxiana to the Hindu Kush passes. From their homeland east of the Caspian they brought the Vedic pantheon of Indo-European deities, including the Sky-god *Dyaus Pitar* (Roman Jupiter, Greek Zeus), usually associated with *Prithivi Mata,* the Earth-goddess, as the universal parents. But Dyaus Pitar is hardly more than the designation 'Bright-sky', and Prithivi, like most other Vedic goddesses, is but a faint reflection of her heavenly spouse, although a hymn in the Rig-veda (V, 84) is devoted to her as representing Earth.

The Harappa civilisation these Aryans encountered had flourished as a highly organised urban culture from about 2500 BC. It was brought dramatically to an end around 1500 BC by barbarian invaders from the west who sacked Harappa itself on the Ravi rivers and Mohenjo-daro and Chandhu-daro in the Lower Indus valley, and burnt the Baluchi villages. It is uncertain whether we should identify these raiders with the Aryans, or whether the latter invaders settled in cities that had already been destroyed, but there is no doubt that the subsequent culture was a syncretism of the new Indo-European traditions with an earlier, probably Dravidian religion.

The Dravidians, who spoke a non-Aryan language which is the oldest in India, came from the north-west. Originally, they stemmed from the Eastern Mediterranean region and Asia Minor, and they may possibly have links with the ancient Cretans, whose land was for so long the cult-centre of the Mother-goddess. It has been conjectured that two branches of the original race migrated eastwards, one settling in Mesopotamia as the Sumerians, while the others travelled by way of southern Iran and the Makran coast to North-west India. After the Aryan invasion, the Dravidians (known anciently as *Damila*, hence the modern *Tamil*) moved southwards, exercising a profound influence not only on the incoming Aryan language, but on the popular religion of the whole sub-continent. Today the majority of Indians are of Dravidian stock and, particularly in South India, they address their worship to non-Aryan deities. Hinduism is thus a combination of pre-Aryan (Dravidic) and Vedic Aryan elements, and over all the figure of the Mother-goddess looms large.

Throughout India the sanctity of the earth is reckoned paramount, and around its worship the Goddess-cult has found many modes of popular expression. In every village the Earth-mother is represented as the tutelary deity (*grama devata*), revered under various names, such as Mata, Amba, Kali, Rati, and so on. After each successive harvest, the exhausted soil has to be rejuvenated with fertility rites, which in the past included human sacrifices like the *meriah* ritual of the Khonds, noted above (see p. 97). But in general, the cult of the divine Matris, or Mothers, is followed by all the people of each rural Hindu community, apart from the Brahmins, and is particularly observed in times of special hardship, as when the community is being plagued with cholera or smallpox epidemics or similar scourges. The Goddess exercises a fearful control over her people's fortunes, and she can be as malignant as beneficial; to neglect her worship is to invite calamity upon oneself and family.

As representing Mother-earth, her shrine is often in the charge of the womenfolk, or of a non-Brahminic priest drawn from one of the pre-Aryan tribes. In this capacity of life-giver, the Goddess is usually propitious, and her *yoni* or vulva is identified with the furrows in the soil, as we saw above. On the other hand, nowhere is the duality of sexuality, favourable and sinister, more explicit than when the Goddess is portrayed as *Shakti* ('energy'), consort of the god Shiva. Then her cult, *Shakta,* is devoted to the embodiment of the female principle, and in the oldest traditions the Goddess is often given pride of place, being identified with the One, combining the Universal Male with the Universal Female. Shakti overshadows her consort, and her cult, which embraces every aspect of feminine sexuality, is akin to, and often identified with Tantrism, referred to in the last chapter.

Venerated in her maternal character, Shakti is the Mother-goddess, 'whose slender waist, bending beneath the burden of the ripe fruit of her breasts, swells into jewelled hips, heavy with the promise of infinite maternities' (Walker, *Hindu World* ii, p. 336). She can be thus portrayed as the essence of conjugal bliss, in myth as

Shiva's consort, and in more mystical terms, as the expression of sexual joy and desire, the union of Energy and Being, in Tantrism the means to ultimate knowledge. The conjoined sex organs, the male *linga* and the female *yoni*, are the subjects of tantrik meditation, and, in particular, the vulva either in replica or as the living organ of a young, naked virgin, is worshipped as part of the Shakta cult to symbolise eternal virginity.

The more sinister face of Shakti is her *bhairav*, 'terror' aspect; she is then the deity of a death cult. As Kali, Durga, and Bhavani, the Goddess is portrayed in the most repulsive and terrible forms. With 'black' (*kali*) visage, she appears wearing a necklace of human skulls, in two of her four hands she holds a sword and a dagger, and in the other two are severed heads dripping with blood. Her long tongue protrudes from her mouth, and blood trickles down her neck as she gorges herself at cannibal feasts. In one hideous image, a decapitated Kali holds her own severed head, while the mouth greedily drinks the blood spurting from her neck.

Durga similarly relishes the taste of human blood, and is often accompanied by eight demonesses called *yogini* who chew the bones left over after their mistress's gory repasts.

In Tantrism, Shakti as Bhairavi is the essence of universal dread, a manifestation of the 'awesome mysteries of the cosmos, including all life's uncomprehended forces, from the pain of birth and the panic of living to the fearful uncertainties of death'. Her spouse, Shiva, is similarly endowed with a fearsome aspect as Bhairava. In his accredited eight 'terror' shapes, he is described as black-limbed, destructive, wrathful, red-crested, and so on. His companions are ghouls, demons, and ogresses, and his *vahana*, 'vehicle', is a misshapen dog with evil fangs and slavering jaws, who is as terrible to behold as his master. Shiva's sinister qualities are invoked in ceremonial maledictions, and form the subject of meditation by tantrik devotees at graveyards, during necrophilic rites (Walker, *op. cit.*, ii, p. 484).

Many of the Shakta temples have been built in or near cremation grounds and burial places and the cult's followers inhabit such places. Their objects of devotion include representations of Shiva and Shakti (as Kali) in their most repulsive aspects, sometimes featuring them as two emaciated ascetics sitting amid a pile of decaying corpses and dried bones. Again, the serpent theme is much in evidence, Kali being shown wreathed in snakes, holding a skull in her hand and wearing a garland of human heads. Shiva appears as a putrescent corpse with the black Kali sitting astride him, peeling off and eating pieces of his rotting flesh. As she does so, she emits flashes of malignant power like rings of purplish light playing around her head.

The rites of the necrophilic cult (*shavavada*, 'corpse-way') are almost too terrible to contemplate, for they involve a pathological concern with everything that most normal people would find utterly repulsive. The adept believes that if he can override the conventional dictates of ordered society, and his own inborn aversion to the more gruesome aspects of death, he can rise above the laws of men and gods and claim for himself great personal power. Above all, to kill living beings, and particularly other humans, in the most lingering and painful ways possible, will impart to the devotee special magical abilities and the power to influence his fellow-men.

Neophytes will not only gladly assist in the preparation of corpses for cremation, but they will exhume those that have been buried and eat their rotting flesh, estimating the brain, lungs, and testicles of men especially vitalising. They also seek to have sexual intercourse with corpses in the belief that contact between the adept's penis and the genitals of a dead woman, or the anus of a male corpse, will endow him with occult power. In the so-called Black Rite (*nilasadhana*), the yogi tries to re-animate the dead person by sitting astride the corpse and enacting certain magical rituals.

Distant cries and groans are said to be heard which gradually approach and enter the body. The corpse twitches and struggles, its tongue protrudes horribly, and the yogi cuts it off for future magical use; it is said that its organ erects and that it ejaculates, and the fluid is collected and used. (Walker, *op. cit.*, ii, p. 131.)

Necrophilia, for all the repulsiveness of its perverse sexuality, nevertheless echos a primitive concern in Man for his dead, that is at least as old as the Neanderthal burial rites of seventy thousand years ago (see above, p. 73ff.). The corpse may have surrendered its soul, but even the inert flesh that remains still has within it the material for its regeneration. Restored to the terrestrial womb that gave him birth, the dead person can yet be recreated, and receive anew the vital spark that can never be extinguished.

13

The Word of God

Many strange religio-magical practices have become associated with the cult of the Earth-mother. As Queen of the Underworld she takes on a sombre aspect in mythology, like Hekate of the ancient Greeks, the grim and fantastic mistress of ghosts and witches and therefore of all magic, most of it sinister in intent and execution.

In the Earth's womb were the souls of the dead, awaiting their turn to be clothed with new flesh for rebirth. If those ghosts could be called forth from their infernal ante-chamber and questioned, it was thought that they might be persuaded to divulge some of the mysteries to which their subterranean existence gave them access. For the seat of wisdom was believed to lie in the heart of the earth, depository of the seed of life and knowledge. The reasoning that equated the germ of creation with the divine Word would seem to have proceeded along these lines:

Rain is the spermatozoa of the Earth-mother's heavenly consort, the Sky-god. The most forceful, and thus effective spurting of the seed is accompanied by thunder and the shrieking of the tempest, the voice of the god in the storm-wind. Somewhere above the sky, a mighty penis reaches its climax that shakes the heavens. The lips of the glans open and the sacred juice spurts forth, to be borne by the wind to earth. As saliva can be seen mixed with breath in a man's forceful speech, so the 'speaking' of the divine phallus is accompanied by 'spittle' amid the howling wind.

This 'spittle' is the visible 'Word' of the Creator, the *Logos* of the Greek and Christian philosophers, which 'was with God, and was God, and was in the beginning with God; through whom all things were made, and without him was not anything made that was made. In him was life . . . .' (John 1:1–4). In the words of the biblical psalmists: 'By the word of the Lord the heavens were made, and all their host by the breath of his mouth' (33:6); and, 'When thou sendest forth thy breath they are created, and the face of the earth is restored' (104:30).

However metaphysical this concept of the creative Logos may have become in more sophisticated times, originally it was not an abstract notion; you could see the 'Word of God', feel it as rain on your face, watch it seeping into the furrows of the earth, the 'vulva' of the womb of creation. Beneath the ground lay a great ocean whose waters, like those of the seas around and above the firmament (Genesis 1:7), were the primeval reservoirs of the Creator-father's spermatozoa, the Word, the source of all wisdom. They were therefore known as the 'seas of knowledge' by the ancient Sumerians, and their resources could be tapped by the seekers of truth, whether they looked 'to the heavens or to the earth beneath' (Isaiah 51:6), that is, by means of astrology or necromancy, divination from the dead.

Since it was given to few men to be able to visit heaven or hell and return to tell what they had seen and heard, there arose a class of inspired persons who could dissociate from the everyday world and make direct contact with the source of divine knowledge. Their illumination might be direct, like the mystic who sees the face of God in a vision, or through an intermediary, like the spiritualist medium or the witch, with their 'familiars'.

To raise the spirits of the dead has long been considered a fruitful means of enlightenment. Isaiah speaks scornfully in the Bible of those professing such dark practices as 'chirping and muttering' when they seek their oracles through 'the dead, on behalf of the living' (8:19). The reference is to the incomprehensibility of so many of their messages to the uninitiated. It seems that their ravings must be attributable to some special language reserved for such esoteric communications, whose interpretation could therefore be undertaken only by equally inspired individuals. The enthusiastic 'shamans' of the Early Church had to be reminded that 'speaking with tongues' was of limited benefit to the faithful without an accompanying explanation in ordinary language:

> . . . be zealous for spiritual gifts, especially that you might prophesy. For one speaking in a tongue speaks not to man but to God; for no one understands him, but he utters mysteries in the spirit . . . if you in a tongue utter speech that is not intelligible, how will anyone know what is said? . . . Therefore, he who speaks in a tongue should pray for the power to interpret. . . . If, therefore, the whole Church assembles and all speak in tongues, and outsiders or unbelievers enter, will they not say you are mad? (I Corinthians 14: 1–23.)

which was better, perhaps, than being accused, like the apostles at Pentecost for similar behaviour, of being drunk (Acts 2:13).

The 'new wine' which on that occasion had apparently been suggested as the true inspiration for the apostles' oracular communications, may have had some special cultic significance. It has been pointed out that 'new wine' (Hebrew *tirosh*) was a specific constituent of the ritual meal consumed by the Essenes, those other Jewish sectarians of the time who lived by the Dead Sea; they, also, in their ceremony were commemorating the coming of their Messiah. Certainly, some kind of artificial stimulant has long been a contributory factor in the art of divination and soothsaying, enabling the seer to dissociate at will.

The particular hallucinatory agents employed depend upon local culture and availability. But, in general, the philosophy underlying the peculiar properties of the drug plants is one aspect of the concept concerning the subterranean fount of divine knowledge. Since all plants have their roots below ground and are nourished from the seminal rain above, it follows that all are endowed with some measure of the 'Word of God'. Common experience showed, however, that some of the Earth-mother's offspring are more 'powerful' than others; some plants taste stronger, or have more marked effects for good or ill on the body and on the mind. The distillation from such very special vegetation can put a person to sleep, like the narcotics, or stimulate the nervous system, like the psychotropic drugs. Among these was the Holy Plant, or Sacred Mushroom, which had the effect of alternating bouts of extreme physical and mental activity with periods of deep lethargy. It was reasonable, therefore, to assume that those plants which could affect people so strongly must contain more than the usual amount of divine sperm, the 'Word', or have it in a more concentrated form, and anyone consuming them must be able to assimilate this wisdom directly into his body. Thus stimulatory drugs were considered to have a legitimate place in divinatory techniques and are still so used, in or out of specifically religious contexts. Some modern users of LSD-type, so-called 'sacramental', drugs describe their 'trips' in religious terms, strikingly reminiscent of Prophetic visions recorded in the Bible, such as the chariot imagery in the opening chapters of the Book of Ezekiel, and the Son-of-Man apparition described by St John the Divine, in the Book of Revelation (1:12–16).

Sensual perception is enhanced, colours seem brighter, sounds more intense, and spatial and temporal distances are foreshortened. The subject is sometimes convinced that he has been granted, in one glorious moment of comprehension, the secret of life and the universe, breathtakingly beautiful in its simplicity, and yet only an earnest of the glory that awaits the visionary who perseveres in his quest for the face of God. We may cite as an example the experience of an LSD-user after a 'trip':

> But then in a flash of illumination, I understood that this perfect genius of which I conceived was nothing more than a minute and miserable microcosm, containing but the barest

> hint of the infinitely more complex and enormously vast macrocosmic Mind of God. I knew that for all its wondrous precision this man-mind even in ultimate fulfilment of all its potentials could never be more than the feeblest reflection of the God-Mind in the image of which the man-mind had been so miraculously created. I was filled with awe of God as my Creator, and then with love for God as One Who sustained me even, as in my images, I seemed to sustain the contents of my own mind . . . I marvelled all the more at the feeling I now had that somehow the attention of God was focused upon me and that I was receiving the enlightenment from Him. Tears came into my eyes and I opened them upon a room in which it seemed to me that each object had somehow been touched by God's sublime Presence.

Professor Ioan Lewis, who quotes this instance in his book *Ecstatic Religion* (Harmondsworth, 1971, p. 38), compares it with the reported experience of an Eskimo shaman who sought a similar revelation in the solitude of the wilderness. He had achieved his trance-state through the more traditional techniques of fasting and ascetic meditation, which controlled experiments have shown can produce the same clinical symptoms as the psychedelic agents favoured by the modern 'instant' prophet.

> I soon became melancholy. I would sometimes fall to weeping and feel unhappy without knowing why. Then for no reason all would suddenly be changed, and I felt a great inexplicable joy, a joy so powerful that I could not restrain it, but had to break into song, a mighty song, with room for only one word; joy, joy! And I had to use the full strength of my voice. And then in the midst of such a fit of mysterious and overwhelming delight I became a shaman, not knowing myself how it came about. But I was a shaman. I could see and hear in a totally different way. I had gained my enlightenment, the shaman's light of brain and body, and this in such a manner that it was not only I who could see through the darkness of life, but the same bright light also shone out for me, imperceptible to human beings but visible to all spirits of earth and sky and sea, and these now came to me to become my helping spirits. (*op. cit.*, p. 37.)

All the old oracles of repute were inspired by the Earth-mother. One of the most famous, at Delphi, was served by the Goddess's priestess, called the *Pythia,* or

Pythoness. She sat on a tripod over the Omphalos, a rounded stone marking the centre or 'navel' of the earth. It has been suggested that a large measure of her inspiration came from certain intoxicating vapours that arose from a cleft in the ground at that point, rather as the highly aromatic fumes of the priestly oil of anointing were probably intended to have a similar effect on the attendants at Yahweh's shrine in ancient Israel (Exodus 30: 30–38). The oracular utterances of the Pythia were so incoherent to her clients that it became customary for priestly interpreters to be in constant attendance at the shrine to 'translate' the Goddess's words into classical hexameters. In fact, this intrusion of masculine influence into what was primarily a feminine province had probably more to do with the extension of patriarchal political control over the land, following on the Achaean and Dorian invasions of the thirteenth and twelfth centuries BC, than the exigencies of oracular communication.

At Dodona, in Epirus near modern Jenina, another famous oracle was associated with the Earth-goddess, personified in this case as Dione. Her prime role in the cult was later usurped by her consort Zeus, but this masculine influence was again almost certainly secondary. The oracle centred upon sacred oak trees which were believed to reveal the deity's will by the sound of rustling in the leaves, as Yahweh instructed his servant David in battle tactics with the sound of 'sighing' in the tops of the poplars (I Chronicles 14:15). A closer connection with the earth at Dodona is suggested by the tradition that the priests attending the oracle were required to sleep on the soil, and to walk barefoot in order to maintain contact at all times with the powerful emanations from the ground. The fertility associations of the cult were clearly demonstrated by the discovery during excavations at the site of a mass of archaic bronze figurines of stock-animals, doubtless devoted by local farmers to the deity in intercession for their herds' fecundity.

We have already referred to the peculiar nature of the Dead Sea area whose comparative depth brought it into a uniquely close relationship with the womb of the earth and its subterranean fires. It may be significant that the Essenes chose to live out their ascetic lives in that part of the Judaean Wilderness. They were famed for their supposed ability to foretell the future with remarkable accuracy, and were believed to have power of evil spirits. They certainly practised astrology, as we know from their scrolls. One fragmentary document, painstakingly inscribed in a coded alphabet, purports to outline the effects on the body and mind of a subject's birth within the influence of zodiacal 'houses' (see Allegro, *The Dead Sea Scrolls,* Harmondsworth, 1964, p. 127). It is not impossible that this occultist society practised necromancy also, but unfortunately we are never likely to learn the full extent of their 'mysteries', since their innermost secrets were transmitted between teachers and novices only by word of mouth, and under the most fearsome oaths of confidentiality. The sect's quest for the 'knowledge of God' formed an essential part of their religion, as we know, and whatever this phrase signified in any particular instance, their biblical interpretations were much concerned with relating the events of their day with biblical prophecy as indicators towards the expected commencement of the millenium.

Strictly speaking, prophecy in the religious sense includes every aspect of divine revelation, imparting spiritual truths about God and the universe. It has, however, become more popularly applied to that part of divine wisdom relating to the future, prognostication of the kind illustrated in the biblical story of King Saul, when he inquired from the ghost of the prophet Samuel the likely outcome of the following day's battle.

The popularity of fortune-telling cults in every age is a measure of Man's emotional insecurity. He can only feel sure of himself if he can be convinced that there is a divine plan in which he has an essential part to play. So much aspiration to the 'knowledge of God' is aimed at securing that assurance, and discovering the nature and limits of the suppliant's role. On a less elevated level, the anxious inquirer of his fate in the ever-popular astrology features in our newspapers demonstrates a similar faith that each person's propensities in deed and decision are pre-ordained for him by the juxtaposition of the planets at his birth. Thereafter his course of conduct is likely to be most advantageous when limited within those boundaries of inclination, and the imaginative journalists who compile these columns will sketch out carefully ill-defined areas where their readers might expect their efforts to meet with particular difficulty or success.

Underlying this conception of God's unfolding plan for the individual is the conviction that time, as we understand it, is a relative dimension, and meaningful only within the limited comprehension of mortals. Beyond Man's span of understanding, all past, present, and future is arrayed in one cohesive pattern that gives creation its form and purpose. Our mathematicians are struggling to rediscover this concept of relativity in arithmetical terms, but for its philosophical origin we should again look back to Man's long history as a child of nature.

Long before he was able to plan ahead, to stay his hand against the urging of his immediate desires, Man shared with the other animals an instinctive empathy with the seasonal rhythms of the natural world. What happened today was an echo from the past; the pattern of tomorrow had been laid in previous seasons. There was a balance and repetitiveness in nature which provided her creatures with their biological time-keeping, telling them when to hibernate, or spawn, or migrate to warmer climates. It is only when Man developed his imagination and dared to challenge his environment instead of adapting to it, that he needed to flout his instinctive chronometry with unseasonable behaviour. As a hunter he tracked his quarry into ice-belts that should have frozen him to death. Hunger, greed, or sheer curiosity lured him from the comparative security of his familiar haunts to journey vast distances into the unknown. Then, faced with unfamiliar perils in hostile climates, he began to doubt the future. The regular unfolding of the seasons had been disrupted; climatic variations and unusual ecological conditions demanded his continual reassessment of the situation and planned counteraction. His very survival depended upon a series of urgent estimates of likely hazards. He no longer felt confident of nature's providence. Nothing was predictable; tomorrow was unknown, and fearful. The stage was now set for the lucrative business of the astrologer, interpreter of dreams and tea-leaves, readers of bumps on the head and creases in the skin, and all that mighty army of clairvoyants who, for a price, will reassure us by unrolling the scroll of destiny another pathetic inch or two.

It also called for a religion which looked to a deity who stood outside the fragmented time-cognisance of Man and could offer him a faith in an eternity which made sense of life, and raised its horizons beyond the mortal span of three-score years and ten.

14

The Witch-Hunt

Thou shalt not suffer a witch to live.

(*Exodus* 22:18)

If the mysterious power that women possess could generate new life, it followed that it might also be used to harm and destroy. The Mother-goddess, as the supreme expression of the feminine principle, could therefore be worshipped as a war-deity. The 'Virgin Anat' of the Bronze-Age pantheon of ancient Canaan is portrayed in her epic as a bloody warrior wading thigh-deep in her enemies' blood. Aphrodite, whom the Romans identified with their Venus, was a patroness of war as well as of love, beauty, and marriage. Athene also leads her people into battle when she is not overseeing the more domestic arts of cooking, weaving, and spinning.

The belief that women were able to exercise their influence in a malign fashion gave ready credence to tales of witches, those especially gifted females who could not only command the spirits of the dead, like the medium of Endor, but direct the thoughts and actions of the living. They were credited with blighting crops, causing pregnant animals to miscarry, making wives barren and husbands impotent; they sucked the blood of children and ate their flesh in the unholy concourses; they flew by night on broomsticks, or on the backs of animals who served them as their attendant spirits, or familiars.

There is a remarkable similarity between the reputed powers and practices of the European witches, who were subjected to such terrible persecution during the Middle Ages, and those in Africa whose hounding by self-appointed witch-hunting cults has been of more recent times. In both places the supposed witches were mainly women, and their persecutors men, and in both the witch-hunts occurred during periods of social disruption when traditional centres of authority were weakened through wars, plagues, or the intrusion of alien customs and cultures. Such disturbances bring to hitherto closely-knit communities a general sense of insecurity and estrangement that can too easily develop into a paranoiac hunt for scapegoats.

In Europe, the power and teachings of the Christian Church played a special part in the beginning and development of the persecutions. After a millenium or so of ecclesiastical rule and growing corruption, a number of reform movements were taking hold among the common people and threatening to undermine the Church's authority. Its leaders were becoming increasingly nervous of 'heresies', like the Cathari ('pure ones') and the Waldensians (followers of Waldo). As usual with such schismatic movements we know little of their true nature and doctrines but have to rely upon the condemnatory records of their detractors. But it is clear that, however justified or otherwise the Church's hostility, these sects enjoyed a great deal of popular support. In the thirteenth century the new preaching orders of the Church, in particular the Dominicans, were given the duty of seeking out and exposing the heretics wherever they might be found, and bringing them to book. So began the infamous activities of the Inquisition with its terrifying armoury of tribunals, secret police, informers, tortures, and fiery executions.

Many of the accusations levelled against the schismatics we may recognise as those customarily directed at witches: the Cathari were said to ride to their unholy meetings on broomsticks or poles anointed with oil, or to worship the Devil who appeared to them in monstrous forms. They were said to live licentiously, and reverence their own appointed leaders above all other men, while denying the Church its rightful dues in honour and taxes.

Faced with doctrinal dissension from within, the Church had also to counter the devastating effects of natural disasters like the bubonic plague, or Black Death, which ravaged Europe in the fourteenth century. By 1350, when it had spread to England, the plague had already carried off about a third of the population of Europe. If the finger of responsibility for God's wrath were not to be pointed at the Church and its deficiencies, some other scapegoats had to be found.

It was the Jewish population that was first sacrificed on the altar of public indignation. They were accused of various crimes, including the eating of the flesh of unbaptised children on their Sabbath, again like the witches. Most of the Jews in Germany were exterminated, and those who escaped fled eastwards to Poland and Russia.

Since the plague occurred every ten years or so, fresh victims were required when the Jews had been annihilated or driven away. The Church's princes had long cast envious eyes upon the power and wealth of the Knights Templar, gained as a result of their Crusades against the Moslem infidel. Now seemed the time to voice suspicion that the faith of these Christian warriors had been corrupted by their over-zealous association with the mystic East, and that they had become dabblers in the occult. Could they not have thereby changed their allegiance from God to the Devil, and thus brought about the ills that had befallen Christendom?

At the beginning of the fourteenth century, Philip IV of France launched an attack against the Order. Before long, his Inquisitors had produced the 'evidence' they sought. The Templars were convicted on their own tortured admission that they had denied Christ, worshipped the Devil in animal form, roasted children and used their fat to anoint idols, kissed their superiors' bodies in the most obscene and improbable places, and, in general, perpetrated all the horrific deeds associated with witchcraft.

In due course, when the sacrificial possibilities of the Templars and their wealth were also exhausted, the Inquisitors turned their attention to those defenceless females who were to become the main victims of the witch-hunts. In the fifteenth century, witchcraft was separated from the crimes of sorcery and black magic and removed from the jurisdiction of the secular courts. Now persons so accused were handed over to the Church's Inquisitors for examination and condemnation.

It was not difficult to persuade the desperately troubled people of Europe that most of their ills could be attributed to the secret practices of a few crones living in their midst. The poorer, older, and lonelier the women, the easier it was to suspect them of being witches. It was now a common belief that such persons flew by night to join their companions in their sinister concourses, there to indulge in eating human flesh and jointly exerting terrible powers of fascination against anyone unfortunate enough to cross their path.

The poor wretches were dragged from their hovels and, in effect, offered the choice between confessing immediately to the most bizarre and unlikely crimes and practices and so hastening their immediate, if agonising, end at the stake, or submitting to the most brutal tortures before confessing, with the same unhappy end. Needless to say, the only limit to the tale of their misdeeds was the scope of their Inquisitors' imaginations. It was wide enough; Pope Innocent VIII's own delegates, his 'dear sons' Heinrich Kramer and Jakob Sprenger, Professors of Theology, of the Order of Friars Preachers, produced in 1486 a notorious manual of procedure for witchcraft trials called *Malleus Maleficarum*, 'the Hammer of Witches', which has been reckoned one of the most obscene books ever written. Sprenger, its chief author, was a dangerous and evil-minded fanatic, who revelled in recounting every form of sexual deviation and gross indecency that he and his informants could conceive in their own twisted minds.

The trials were a mockery of justice; tortures were devised that could be prolonged into days of agony, children were persuaded to denounce their parents, evidence was accepted from convicted criminals, and anyone who spoke in the victim's defence was automatically suspected of complicity in her crimes. The ultimate cynicism of the whole degrading procedure was that the Church maintained her innocence of the final act of judicial murder by handing over the broken, whimpering bodies of her victims to the secular authority for the fiery *coup de grâce*.

There were some protests, of course. So many of the 'confessions' were too obviously obtained under duress, the deeds recounted so improbable, that more level-headed jurists argued that the craft itself must be quite illusory, its professed activities no more than the deluded fancies of lunatics. They claimed as their ecclesiastical authority a decree of about AD 900, and dubiously attributed to the obscure fourth-century Council of Ancyra, to be known later by the theologians as the *canon episcopi* (Gratian's *Decreta* 2.26.5 12). This linked witchcraft with the classical goddess Diana/Artemis, declaring:

> Some wicked women, following Satan's provocations and seduced by the illusions and phantasms of demons, believe and profess that they ride at night with Diana, the pagan goddess . . . on certain beasts, with an innumerable company of Women, passing over immense distances, obeying her commands, as their mistress, and evoked by her on certain nights. . . . Therefore, priests everywhere should preach that they know this to be false, and that such phantasms are sent by the Evil Spirit, who deludes them in dreams. Who is there who is not led out of himself in dreams, seeing much in sleeping that he never saw waking? And who is such a fool that he believes that to happen in the body which is done only in the spirit?

The decree seems to have carried considerable weight

at the time; it became part of the Church's canon law and it was doctrinally not permissible thereafter to believe in the reality of night-flying. Nevertheless, this conviction that witches fly, often at night and over long distances, has been one of the most widespread and enduring of all beliefs associated with the craft. Indeed, magic flight on sticks, animals, or carpets, is a common feature of folklore generally. Popular Hindu religion knows of witches using spells to fly themselves to their nocturnal gatherings. Medieval Judaism speaks of women with long, flowing hair, flying by night to such meetings, no doubt recalling the common, if etymologically false, association of the biblical *Lilith*, the desert demon (Isaiah 34:14; etc.) with the Hebrew word for 'night' (*lailah*). In Africa, tradition abounds with stories of witches who fly to their assignations as nightjars, bats, owls, and fireflies.

The phallic nature of the 'broomstick' theme is easily discernible, especially in such confessions as these, elicited by the sixteenth-century Inquisitor, Henry Boguet:

> François Secretain said that, to go to the Sabbat, she placed a white wand between her legs and uttered certain words, and that she was then conveyed through the air. . . . Thievenne Paget said that the first time the Devil appeared to her, it was in full daylight in the form of a big black man, and that when she had given herself to him, he embraced her and raised her in the air and conveyed her to the house in the field of Longchamois (*An Examen of Witches*, 1590, tr. E. A. Ashwin, London, 1929, p. 41).

The sensation of 'floating' is, again, not uncommon among women in sexual orgasm, but it is also significant that witches often claimed that their ability to fly was due to some special ointment that they first smeared over their naked bodies:

> Some rub themselves first with a certain ointment, and others use none. There are also some who are not witches, but after anointing themselves do not fail to fly up through the chimney and to be carried away as if they were witches. (Boguet, p. 44.)

Certainly the feeling of 'flying' is one we have all experienced in our dreams, and it is said to be one of the common effects of certain hallucinatory drugs, the subjects reporting afterwards that it seemed to them that they were flying over vast distances. One is reminded of prophetic visions that include such experiences, like that of Ezekiel who was 'lifted up by the Spirit between earth and heaven' and brought 'in the visions of God' to Jerusalem from his place of exile in Mesopotamia (8:3), and that of Muhammad who was conveyed by night to the divine presence where he communed with Allah face to face:

> Glory be to Him who journeyed by night with his servant from the Sacred Mosque (i.e. the Ka'aba at Mecca) to the Furthest Mosque (i.e. the Temple at Jerusalem) around which we have bestowed blessing, that We might show him some of Our Signs . . . (Qur'an 17:1.)

In an appendix to Margaret Murray's book, *The Witch-cult in Western Europe* (Oxford, 1921), Professor A. J. Clark examines three of the cited formulae for 'flying ointments', and notes that one of them contains aconite and belladonna (Deadly Nightshade), which would induce both excitement and irregular heart action. He says that the latter symptom in a person falling asleep 'produces the well-known sensation of falling through space, and it seems quite possible that the combination of a delirifacient like belladonna with a drug producing irregular action of the heart, like aconite, might produce the sensation of 'flying' (p. 280f.).

Eventually the European nightmare ended. Enlightened scientific and medical opinion grew less inclined to ascribe all unusual phenomena to diabolical influence. A reformed Church recovered some humanity along with its sanity, and from the seventeenth century its leaders became increasingly obliged to acknowledge the opinions of scientifically-minded thinkers among even its own ranks. In 1736, the English Parliament repealed the law that required a condemned witch to be put to death, albeit in the face of a good deal of popular opposition: thirty-two years later, John Wesley, founder of the Methodist communion, could still express his regret that 'the English in general, and indeed most of the men of learning in Europe, have given up all accounts of witches and apparitions as mere old wives' fables'. As late as 1946, the over-credulous writer on witchcraft, Montague Summers, found the *Malleus Maleficarum* a 'noble treatise' and a 'very great and wise book' (*Witchcraft and Black Magic*, London [Arrow ed.] pp. 9, 25).

In Africa, witchcraft is still an important part of village life, and even in larger communities where education is spreading, belief in the powers of witches holds considerable sway. Where the farmer might fear that his barren field or sow is under the influence of a hostile spirit directed by a witch, so the student who fails his examinations, or the unsuccessful businessman will also suspect some similarity directed malign power.

A number of features appearing in African witchcraft are common to those we have seen obtaining in medieval Europe. Witches fly by night, meet in assemblies of their own kind, eat human flesh, dance naked in secret places and rob the graves of their dead for diabolical purposes. They have the power of causing barrenness in women and impotence in men, destroy crops, cut off and consume certain parts of their victims' bodies, and suck their blood. They have familiars, like owls, snakes, and hyenas, and sometimes change themselves into such creatures, or are taken over by their spirits to the point where they may lose all control.

Some tribes believe that witches possess some material substance in their bodies which contains the source of their special power. The Azande, who live on the Nile–Congo divide, believe the substance can be revealed in a post-mortem examination, and that it is inherited by the witches' children. The Tiv people of central Nigeria speak of a witchcraft-substance called *tsav* which grows on the hearts of some humans and animals. It is said to look like the liver, but it is smaller and may be rounded or notched at the edges. It is coloured red, black, or white, and is capable of exerting a good or bad influence.

The possessor of this powerful substance may not be aware of its presence in the body, but its fruits will be evident from his powerful personality and material prosperity. In a part of the world where longevity is not normal, it follows from the mere fact of their survival that long-lived individuals must be endowed with this gift. They are thus potentially dangerous, since possession of *tsav* gives that person the power to bewitch others, to send them evil dreams, and to concoct deadly poisons. The presence of an elder at his younger relative's funeral is sufficient to arouse suspicion that he may have been responsible for his kinsman's death.

Not all Africans believe that the witch's special powers reside in some visible organic appendage, or that it can be inherited; but in general the ability to influence others from afar is widely credited to some vital force that witches possess beyond the measure enjoyed by ordinary mortals. It is this spiritual energy that is seen as the common factor in all religion and magic, and it can reside in plants and animals as well as human beings. In terms of the old fertility philosophy, we might say that it is a measure of the volume and purity of the creator-god's spermatozoa that all organisms receive during their gestation in field or womb. As some plants have the power to kill or revive, and some animals are more fierce or fleet than others, so especially endowed humans possess some unusual faculty that enables them to achieve success themselves or to control the fortunes of their fellows.

The Ghanaian believes that a witch can use her powers to increase her own prosperity or to ensure that of her clients. But the affluent farmer needs to beware lest his success bring upon him the suspicion that his accomplishments are due to supernatural influences, generated either from within himself or by his recourse to a witch. At least, in this case, the vital force has been used for good; the danger is that it can be equally diverted to evil ends and the hurt of the witch's enemies. Furthermore, were this to happen, the witch herself will be thereafter tainted with the malignity she has herself projected; she can no longer be a force for good in the community, but must be exposed and her power neutralised.

If African witchcraft reflects many of the features we have found in the European cults, so, unhappily, do attempts at its extirpation. Exposing the activities of supposed witches has become a major concern of certain religious movements, claiming that they thereby remove superstitious fear from the minds of simple people. Their methods are often hardly less disquieting than the evils they denounce. Young Africans, dressed in European clothes, travel about in twos and threes, summoning local assistance at each place they visit. They call on the local chief to gather his people together and make them pass before them. The self-styled witch-seekers then identify their victims by various magical means. In the 1930s such a cult swept across Nyasaland, Northern and Southern Rhodesia, and into the Belgian Congo. They called themselves Bamucapi, and asserted that they could recognise witches from their reflections in small mirrors. Anyone accused was required to drink a magic potion, a reddish, soapy powder that had to be mixed in a bottle of water. Drinking the liquid was supposed to sap the witch's powers, and also guaranteed the removal of witchcraft from the whole area. If any witch reverted to his evil ways after drinking the potion, he would die and his body would swell up to an enormous size, making it impossible for his mourners to carry it to the grave for decent burial. These potions and other protective charms and powders were sold under the claim that they would afford protection from snake-bites, wild animals, pests, and other misfortunes. More expensive items could also be purchased, guaranteeing the owner special favours from government officials.

A similar operation was mounted in West Africa after the Second World War, and had considerable success, spreading from the Gold Coast to Togoland and Dahomey, and into Nigeria. It came to be known as the Atinga, and its methods were reminiscent of the Bamucapi. Small groups of men would arrive in a village and pay a call on the chief. When the populace had been gathered in an open space, trance-inducing dances were performed by the witch-hunters, after which they were supposed to be inspired with the power of discerning witches. In this case only women were examined, and the ecstatic dancers pointed their lances at their victims, mostly crones. They were made to confess their crimes and to drink a potion to purge their magical powers. Those who refused to confess were forced to undergo an ordeal which, not surprisingly, involved the payment of a fee to the chief Atinga. The woman had also to bring along a chicken and some gin. The Atinga poured a little of the gin on to an altar, and cut the chicken's throat halfway across so that it could run about for a short while before collapsing. If it came to rest with its breast uppermost, the sacrifice was considered to have been accepted by the god and the woman proved innocent. Any other position proved her guilt. In that case, the accused could try again with another fowl, provided she contributed a further donation to the witch-seeker's expenses. If the poor woman still remained uncleared, and refused to confess, or could afford no more chickens or fees, she suffered the fate of her European sisters and was tortured, and in a few cases even beaten to death.

When the cult was finally banned by Government decree, howls of protest were heard throughout the area. The witch-hunting hysteria, once aroused, is self-generating, and by then many people in authority had a vested interest in continuing the practice. Not a few had made a sizeable investment in the purchase of Atinga expertise and were setting up in business as witch-seekers on their own account.

An old witch-hunting cult exists in the Nupe country of Northern Nigeria, called *Ndako gboya* ('ancestor *gboya*'). Its adepts disguise themselves in very tall cylinders of cloth up to fifteen feet high, secured to a pole by which the operator holds the contraption aloft. Strips of coloured cloth fastened to the cylinder flap in the wind as it is paraded among the villagers, the man inside moving his pole up and down for added effect. Three or four of these masked figures, representing ancestral spirits, move around the village, coercing the people to gather in an open space to witness a ceremonial dance performed to the accompaniment of drums. At night the performance reaches a climax and the witch-hunt begins in earnest. No woman is safe from the all-seeing ancestral spirits. The huge masked figures will suddenly turn aside from their dance and bend menacingly over some trembling female. Their assistants rush forward and drag her off into the bush where she is made to undergo an ordeal. With bare hands, she is made to claw the ground until blood begins to ooze from her fingertips: this is a sign of her guilt. In the past she was then held to ransom and put to death if the considerable sum were not immediately forthcoming. More recently she has simply been banished from her home and village.

In those earlier times it was particularly profitable to hold the *Ndako gboya* witch-hunts at harvest-time, since money was then more plentiful to pay the ransoms. Since the profits were shared with the local emir, there was little inclination on his part to discourage the cult. At length, the scandalous business reached such proportions that the central government was forced to ban the *Ndako gboya* from Nupe. However, the society merely extended its activities to other fields and the cult spread far beyond its original frontiers. It was said in 1958 that the movement still flourished in the neighbouring Yoruba country, and that its gowned and hooded practitioners had been seen parading through the modern city of Ibadan (see G. Parrinder, *Witchcraft*, Harmondsworth, 1958, p. 172).

Central governments and religious missions have done their best to combat witchcraft by more legal means and through propaganda, with the avowed intention of saving simple folk from their native superstitions. In fact, much of the unease which nourishes these cults stems from the infiltration of European ideas and customs which have weakened local traditions and tribal authority. The increasing feelings of insecurity among disillusioned and often dispossessed native populations, have given witchcraft added impetus, and prompted the growth of the witch-seeking cults which are threatening the traditional role of the local witch-doctor.

Contrary to much popular misconception, the witch-doctor is not a witch; he is a witch-finder and a professional neutraliser of her baneful influence. He has always been the natives' first recourse for help when they feel threatened from some source of evil in the community. But unlike the European Inquisitors, this seek-and-destroy mission is not his only function; he is a real 'doctor', reassuring his psychologically-disturbed clients in ways they understand and trust.

The witch-doctor possesses many of the attributes of the witch, especially that vital force by which she casts her spells. But it is understood that he will use it only for good; were he to direct it to the furtherance of his own interests, it would turn back against himself and make him no better than those he seeks to expose. Like the witch, he is credited with prescience. He combines the dual functions of the Old Testament prophet in both foretelling the future, and offering reassurance to the anxious souls who seek his help. With that same power of divination he can recognise the source of disturbing influences in his community and, by exposing the person responsible, render her power harmless.

Witches are traditionally required to recognise others of their kind, since they generate their power in meetings strictly reserved for fellow-initiates, like the old Asiatic mystery religions. The adepts have certain outward signs of recognition by which they may know their fellows. It sometimes takes the form of an aura surrounding the witch, visible only to those similarly distinguished. But perhaps more realistically, we should credit the witch-doctor with a shrewd understanding of human nature in general, and the personal characters and motivations of his village neighbours in particular. By careful probing of their anxieties and complaints he can judge the likely source of their troubles.

Nevertheless, some public display of witch-seeking is a psychological necessity, and its effectiveness rests largely upon the power of auto-suggestion. Theoretically, the witch-doctor must first arouse his own latent 'witch-power' by means of a ritual dance in full regalia, accompanied by all the psychedelic paraphernalia of drums, clapping, and flickering fire-light. In the tense atmosphere of anticipation and mounting excitement, he will go into a trance and become a vehicle for his controlling spirits. They will tell him where to point the accusing finger, for now, as one similarly possessed, he shares the witch's powers of mutual recognition.

It is not difficult to understand the effect this performance must have upon a person who, for some reason, suspects she may be the 'guilty' party. Obliged to witness the proceedings, since her absence might be considered a tacit admission of guilt, the 'witch's' nervous apprehension would grow with the acceleration of the drumbeat and the accompanying clapping of the spectators, and the increasing frenzy of the witch-doctor's dance, until the climax of occusation when it came would be almost a relief, and probably precipitated by the reactions of the 'witch' herself.

Which raises the question of why such women have

confessed in Europe and Africa to the most improbable beliefs and practices, and why their statements have met with so large a measure of acceptance, even by those who have known them intimately. Of course, most of the European witches were made to confess under the most hideous forms of compulsion. But not all were tortured, and the African witch-seekers do not normally resort to such drastic methods. Again the extreme nature of so many of the admissions made to the Inquisitors originated largely from the prompting of the examiners themselves, and stemmed from their own lurid and twisted imaginations. Nevertheless, the records contain features which are common to this kind of folk-lore the world over, such as the 'flying by night' and 'blood-sucking' motifs.

By such long-standing traditions people have been conditioned to expect 'witches' to have similar characteristics and to act in certain well-defined ways. Thus, to be old, lonely, mentally deranged, and female, would make one out as a likely 'witch' to credulous and suspicious neighbours in advance of any inquiry. When inexplicable misfortunes occur in a superstitious community, suspicion naturally falls upon a victim possessed of these characteristics, as one different from the accepted norm. Since the poor woman is herself as aware as her neighbours of the marks of a witch, she is already halfway to believing herself capable of all the powers attributed to this calling.

It has been observed that witches' confessions have much in common with the statements made by some psychotic patients undergoing examination. The violent deeds they profess are usually quite imaginary, but their sense of guilt is no less real to them, since the fantasies are the projection of their own inner conflicts. The compulsion to confess is the need to find some relief for this tension.

One observer among the Ashanti tribe found this aspect of witch-hunting well illustrated in the case of a woman accused of the most outrageous conduct. She admitted to cannibalism, causing a motor accident, and making another woman barren, and having made her 'confession' to these unlikely crimes, she seemed to find considerable emotional relief. Her arraignment was done in public, and her release from inner tension was apparently shared by the audience. What mattered now was not the likelihood or gravity of the woman's 'sins', but the fact that by her exposure the evil influence in the community had been extirpated and would not thereafter plague good folk. After the 'confession' and its acceptance by the fetish priest, the witch paid her fine and did her penance, and was received back into society.

If a suspected witch among the Nupe of Nigeria persists in her denials, she is constantly hounded with questions until her resolve weakens and she becomes unsure of herself. After all, who knows what terrible things one may have committed in sleep, when the soul leaves the body and takes wing, perhaps to join a coven of similarly-liberated spirits intent on mischief? Certainly, she has to admit under cross-examination that she has dreamt often enough of her enemies and has taken revenge upon them in nightmares. Perhaps, after all, in her disembodied state she *was* a witch. So, in the end, the accused woman resolves her own doubts by confessing at length to everything suggested to her, or agrees to submit to an ordeal which will almost inevitably prove her guilty.

Such public confessions are marked by general excitement, often leading to a state of trance among the observers as well as in the witch-doctor. In such 'hypnoid' states, the mind is extraordinarily susceptible to suggestion, as has been already pointed out. Ideas may then be freely accepted which would in normal circumstances have been summarily rejected. Furthermore, those newly-acquired convictions will persist thereafter with amazing tenacity. It seems that focally-excited centres of the brain behave in such conditions paradoxically: the more unlikely the idea implanted, the stronger it will be held, and the more it is opposed on rational grounds, the more convinced the subject becomes of its truth.

The technique has served the purpose of 'brain-washers' in every age, whether they be espionage organisations, political demagogues, or religious evangelists. It has also been responsible for many of those fervent self-accusations that feature in certain types of Christian 'witness campaigns'. The penitent believer or newly-made convert is bidden to stand forth from the assembled congregation, and, in a highly-charged state of emotion, recount his sinful condition before he knew the power of saving grace. We may compare the following account of a communal soul-baring ceremony among the Ashanti witnessed by the previous observer:

> The sanded floor of the fetish place would be surrounded by almost the whole population of the village. . . . All this was in the heat of the afternoon. Confession was made through the fetish priest, who prompted and questioned the supplicant at intervals. The audience listened intently to each phrase, and in each pause broke into a kind of chanted prayer, beseeching the fetish to accept the confession. (See Parrinder, p. 159.)

The whole gruelling business was punctuated with the priest's urging the accused to remember his sins, and the crowd's insistence that he hold nothing back. Like the revivalist prayer-meeting, the congregations identify themselves with the sinner, and find in his confession and repentance the absolution of their own guilt.

It is said that among the victims of the witch-hunting cults of Africa, many are quite ignorant of their own involvement in witchcraft until the arrival of their accusers in the village. Only a few admitted to having used evil potions against their enemies, but most of the accused agreed that they had been witches, and some confessed to having belonged to witch-guilds. Practically all maintained that they had been responsible for the death of some near-relative, often their own children or grandchildren, usually by a 'spiritual' cannibalism. Significantly, all were glad to have been 'discovered', since they could now consider themselves free of this embarrassing aptitude for sorcery and able to take their places once more in normal society.

One wishes that the confused and anxious witch-hunting mobs of medieval Europe could have found adequate balm for their unease in periodic soul-cleansing ceremonies of this kind, sharing with the penitent her relief at being freed from the Devil's service and her joy at being received back untainted into her community. Unhappily, the demand of the old religion for a blood sacrifice was too strong; a more primitive drive than compassion drove the witch-seekers in their search for scapegoats and carried their victims to the sacrificial pyres. Perhaps behind the ruffled dignity of the Church there loomed the even more compelling mistress whose power the women had usurped, demanding retribution in the blood of her own kin.

15

The Witches' Religion

Even when all the contributory factors of medieval and modern witch-hunting are taken into account, there still remains the question of the validity of the craft itself as a religion. Were the victims of those purges really self-deluded, confused people, persuaded under conditions of extreme suggestibility into believing themselves witches and capable of working magic? Or did they, quite apart from the compulsion of the rack and the public confessional, hold sincerely that they were practising an age-old religion which demanded their loyalty, even to the stake?

The medieval Christian authorities may have been glad of the opportunity afforded by the witch-hunt for diverting attention from the perils of the time and their own inadequacies, but there is no doubt that they were afraid of the cult; their pursuit of the witches was too intense and ruthless for it to have been a mere diversionary exercise. Some hold that the Church was attacking a rival religion, possibly an indigenous cult that preceded Christianity in Europe and which had widespread contributory sources.

It has been shown that there exists a well-known phenomenon in social development whereby well-rooted and popular traditions can become restricted and shrouded in secrecy when the society that preserved them undergoes radical transformation. In Europe, for example, certain pre-Christian religious ideas went underground when urban societies became Christianised. They were still zealously maintained, but within closed circles of sorcerers, so that what may have once been a common practice and mode of thought among ordinary folk, now took on the air of impenetrable mystery. The secrets were henceforth transmitted to adepts only on the understanding of strict confidentiality.

This kind of 'occultation' may preserve ancient traditions, but the restriction of their circulation to a small, privileged circle only arouses the envy and suspicion of those outside, and almost inevitably invites persecution. Then, when the cult's numbers are reduced and their leaders die off, the fount of authoritative teaching dries up, and errors and debasements circulate uncorrected, weakening the authenticity of the original. This may well have happened already in medieval witchcraft, as it has certainly done in more modern revivalist forms.

The late Margaret Murray was among the most convinced protagonists for the antiquity of the witches' religion. She maintained that, despite the late date of the medieval records and their lack of objectivity in reporting details of the cult, there exists sufficient evidence to support the view that witchcraft did indeed preserve the elements of a very old faith, the

> ancient religion of Western Europe. The god, anthropomorphic or theriomorphic [i.e. appearing in human or animal form] was worshipped in well-defined rites; the organisation was highly developed; and the ritual is analogous to many other ancient rituals . . . it was a developed religion with beliefs, rituals, and organisation as highly developed as any other cult in the world. (*Witchcraft in Western Europe*, 1921, p. 12.)

Dr Murray held that witchcraft began as a matriarchal religion whose chief figure was the Mother-goddess, worshipped mainly by women. In this case, the medieval records must portray a later version of the cult in which a male god has superseded the goddess, as happened elsewhere when a patriarchal culture overran an earlier matriarchal society. The witches speak mainly of a god, identified with the Devil. When he does appear in female form, it is usually as a familiar or substitute for the god, and may be referred to as the 'Queen of the Faerie', or the 'Elfin Queen'.

It has long been suggested that witches and fairies of popular mythology have a common origin in an actual race of small-statured people who formed the indigenous Stone Age population of Northern and Western Europe. According to this theory, they were driven by successive invasions to the less fertile parts of their countries, the inhospitable northern territories, the mountains, or to the open heaths and moors, where they lived in crude mound-dwellings. Since they could only survive by avoiding contact with invaders as far as possible, the 'dwarfs' ventured forth only when it seemed safe to do so, chiefly at night. The newcomers thus knew very little about the people they had displaced and, as always with strangers in an alien land, they tended to regard local beliefs and customs as darkly mysterious, and the 'little people' of the wild places as 'queer folk', endowed with supernatural powers. Their deity seemed to be an embodiment of all that was sinister and evil, worshipped only in great secrecy and under cover of darkness.

Whatever the explanation of its occultism, if the witches' religion did indeed preserve some genuine aspects of a pre-Christian faith, this would certainly go some way to explain the degree of antagonism that could so easily be aroused against its adepts in the witch-hunts. Many of its persecutors were, after all, people who held no particular brief for the established Church of the time, and who were as hostile to the papal legates as they seemed to be towards the old women and little children they watched burning in their market-places.

Any reconstruction of the primitive religion underlying witchcraft must today depend upon an analysis of the medieval records left by its detractors, and upon comparison with existing cult-practices in Africa and elsewhere. The craft is not without its followers today in Europe, and it has, indeed, recently enjoyed a measure of renewed support, largely through the publicity given to its activities by popular writing and television documentaries. Not surprisingly, these have tended to concentrate upon those aspects of the cult that could be expected to titillate the mass palate, particularly the nudism and sexuality of its coven rites. The adherents themselves are usually more reserved about their beliefs, holding that the craft's innermost secrets are not for public knowledge; but whether these represent an unbroken tradition preserved intact over hundreds or even thousands of years, as the witches claim, is at least doubtful.

Certain basic ideas do seem to emerge from a detailed study of the documentary evidence available, and upon these Dr Murray and her sympathisers have tried to reconstruct a picture of the old 'Dianic' cult, so named after the classical goddess Diana, acclaimed by many witches as their deity.

As one might expect, the underlying interest in a predominantly feminine religion was the fertility of the natural world and, in particular, its pastoral rather than agricultural aspects, to judge from the timing of its chief calendrical festivals held on May Eve (30 April, Rood Day) and November Eve (31 October, Allhallow Eve), neither of them particularly significant for farming or the solstices. The rites were centred upon various dances performed by the assembled companies under the leadership of their god, incarnated for the occasion in human or animal form.

Much of the reputed satanic associations of witchcraft seem to derive from the confusion that has arisen in Christian minds about the identity of the witches' god. He is called the Devil, even when he appears in female guise, and so was immediately identified by the medieval clerics with Satan, Lucifer, Beelzebub, the Foul Fiend, and so on, expressing the principle of evil in the universe and the enemy of Man and the Christian God. But to the witches he was not the great destructor, but the Creator of life; they adored him on their knees, addressed their prayers to him as the giver of food and the necessities of life; they dedicated their children to his service, and sacrificed to him. He was not a remote god, for when incarnate he led them in their feasts and dances, and generally shared in what appears to have been a joyful and outgoing religion, characteristics one might expect from a cult that had its origins in the adoration of the Earth-mother in her more benign aspect of the goddess of creation and birth.

The flesh-and-blood 'Devil' of the witches' Sabbath festivals has therefore probably to be understood as the local Chief or Grand Master, generally a man, but occasionally a woman, appearing in some kind of disguise, but recognisable to his followers by a special manual gesture, a password, or a token carried on his person. In this human being the god was believed to have become flesh, and he therefore commanded the homage and obedience of all present. There was often a 'vice-Devil', younger than the Chief, who probably succeeded him on his death and may have been appointed to the office by a council of elders or district officers, themselves designated by the Grand Master.

We may suppose that when the Devil is reported to have appeared before his followers as an animal, the leader was wearing or carrying some token by which his adopted guise might be signified, such as a mask, a skin thrown over his shoulders, or bearing horns fixed to his hat or helmet. The place taken by animals in the cult, whether as the god himself or as familiars in the service of individual witches, does seem to indicate some kind of early animal worship which is, again, what one might well expect from an original pastoral society. We are reminded of the picture of the Stone Age shaman or sorcerer engraved upon the wall of the Three Brothers cave in the Pyrenees. He is similarly arrayed in an animal's skin and a deer's antlers, and appears to be leading some ritual fertility or hunting dance.

Dr Murray points out that dressing up as an animal was considered a heinous offence by the Church as early as the seventh century which, again, signifies that some earlier religion centred upon the adoration of an animal god was still alive at that time, and regarded as a threat to the new faith:

> If anyone at the kalends of January goes about as a stag or a bull; that is, making himself into a wild animal and dressing in the skin of a herd animal, and putting on the heads of beasts; those who in such wise transform themselves into the appearance of a wild animal, penance for three years, because this is devilish. (From the *Liber Poenitentialis* of Theodore, Archbishop of Canterbury, AD 668–690; quoted Murray, p. 21.)

The bestial forms adopted by the Devil in medieval accounts include the bull, and are otherwise most commonly the cat, dog, goat, horse, and sheep.

One of the deity's characteristics was apparently the coldness of his body. This is commented upon by a number of witches who confessed to having come into physical contact with him during the course of their Sabbath rites, not least in the kissing of his posterior, which seems to have been a common gesture of homage. In 1590 at North Berwick, in the words of a contemporary chronicler, Sir James Melville, 'he caused all the company to com and kiss his ers, quilk they said was lyk yce; his body was hard lyk yrn, as they thocht that handled him' (*Memoirs*, p. 395); which suggests that the Devil's ritual disguise covered his entire body, and that it was the cold and hard leather that the devotees touched rather than the flesh of the man beneath.

Where the same chilly description is applied to the Devil's genitals by those women who admitted having had sexual intercourse with him, it seems probable that they had encountered the touch and thrust of an artificial phallus of the kind that has been an object of adoration in mystery religions for thousands of years, the world over. Clay phalli have been found in the Palaeolithic caves of Europe along with figurines of the Mother-goddess, as we noted above (p. 128). Veneration of the male organ was known in the Indus civilisation that preceded the coming of the Aryans, so its recurrence in the cult of the Hindu god Shiva occasions no surprise. Provision is made for the worship of phallic-shaped stones and, although the Rig-veda speaks contemptuously of those 'whose deity is the phallus', by the Epic period the adoration of the *linga* had become an established part of Aryan worship.

Smaller phalli of more natural size, with symbolic devices carved upon them, have long been used in religious sex-rites for simulated copulation; the Roman ithyphallic ('erect penis') god Priapus exercised his rights over the virginity of his young female devotees by having his priests deflower them with such cult objects. The witches' deity claimed similar privileges, and when marriages were arranged within the society, the presiding Devil had real or simulated sexual union with the brides before handing them over to their bridegrooms.

At the major fertility festivals the Devil was required to demonstrate his sexual prowess on a large number of his female followers, which would probably have necessitated recourse to an artificial phallus. This might account for the description of the Devil's organ as very large, rigid, scaly, and cold. The seventeenth-century chronicler, Henri Boguet, records that one of his informants had confessed to having 'grasped the Devil's member many times with her hand, and found it cold as ice' (*Discours des Sorciers,* Lyons, 1608, p. 68f.). Another writer of that time cites other witnesses who variously describe the demonic penis, which was, apparently, usually exposed to view, as being a cubit in length, hanging extended, twisted and sinuous like a serpent, as long and thick as a human arm; of medium thickness, but red, dark, twisted, and very rough and prickly; half iron and half flesh; having the appearance of a horn. Similarly, one Sylvine de la Plaine in 1616 described the Devil's organ as being 'like that of a horse': it 'entered her as cold as ice, and ejaculated semen that was equally chilly, but that on coming out it was glowing as if it had been plunged into a fire' (De Lancre, *L'incredulité et*

Mescréance du Sortilège, Paris, 1662, p. 808). One must presume that the 'semen' was some cold liquid squirted from the phallus at a suitable point in the proceedings to simulate normal seminal ejaculation, in the manner of more elaborate dildos.

One indication that the coupling was not effectual is that pregnancy only followed when the women consented. The coldness of the semen was explained by its 'lacking in vital spirits'; but if the woman was willing to bear the Devil's offspring, copulation took place in a more satisfactory manner, and there is no complaint then of her partner's 'coldness'.

Another indication that the Devil's organ was an artificial contrivance on some occasions is the reports of its causing the female participants some considerable pain during connection. They do seem to have suffered much for their devotion, not only because of the size of their Master's penis, but from its often being 'scaled, like a fish'. At a Sabbath meeting in France, it was said that the Devil took the women behind a screen, and that their children left behind were startled to hear sounds of great distress arising from within. When the women returned from their amorous encounter, they were 'all bloody'. The same is reported of brides who had been prevailed upon to grant the Devil's right to take their virginity; they suffered the loss of a great deal of blood and much pain (Pierre de Lancre, *Tableau de l'Inconstance des mauvais Anges,* Paris, 1613, pp. 219, 404). In these circumstances, it can hardly be maintained that the witches' sex-rites were just sensual orgies, indulged in to sate their carnal appetites.

Nevertheless, not all the fertility festivals of the craft were so painful and sexually unrewarding. There were occasions when the coupling was more natural and unrestrained; at those times the term 'Devil' was applied to any member of the coven, male or female, who acted as a partner in the celebrations. Whatever the religious motive of these symbolic unions, the participants clearly enjoyed themselves, to judge from the accounts given to one Antoinette Bourignon in the seventeenth century by some young witches who had been committed to her charge. They declared that

> they had daily carnal cohabitation with the Devil; that they went to the Sabbaths or Meetings, where they Eat, Drank, Danc'd, and committed other Whoredom and Sensualities. Every one had her Devil in the form of a Man; and the Men had their Devils in the form of a Woman. . . . The had not the least design of changing, to quit these abominable Pleasures, as one of them of Twenty-two Years old one day told me. No, said she, I will not be other than I am; I find too much content in my Condition; I am always Caressed. (*La Parole de Dieu*, 1683: Sir Matthew Hale, *Collection of Modern Relations*, London, 1693, p. 26f.)

Another pert lass of twelve said that she was well acquainted with the Devil: 'he was a Boy a little bigger than herself; and that he was her Love, and lay with her every Night'.

Children were apparently admitted to the revelries from an early age, for another fifteen-year-old girl named Bellot, said that 'her Mother had taken her with her when she was very Young, and that being a little Wench, this Man-devil was then a little Boy too, and grew up as she did, having been always her Love, and Caressed her Day and Night' (*La vie extérieur*, 1683, pp. 211, 214: Hale, pp. 29, 31). This kind of happy relationship could in due course blossom into a witch's marriage, celebrated within the coven, so that a woman's 'Devil' might well be her husband, and *vice versa*.

Dancing played an important part in the witches' festivities, as it has always done in fertility rites. The particular actions involved, the dress of the performers, and the seasons at which the festivals fell, determined the nature of the fertility concerned. There was a 'jumping dance' that seems to have been performed for the encouragement of plant-life; so-called 'obscene dances' were intended to stimulate the fecundity of animals if performed in the appropriate costumes, or of humans if the dancers were not so disguised.

Apart from this, the dances were of two main kinds: those done in a ring, and those of the follow-my-leader type. Both could be led by the Devil, but the ring-dances were often executed around some special object like a large stone, on which the Devil might place himself and play his pipes or other musical instrument. Within those chief categories there appear to have been many different styles of dance. One of some particular interest had the mixed couples dancing back-to-back, gyrating through half-circles at intervals to present each partner in turn to face the exterior of the ring. In Italy, 'the woman was held behind her partner and they danced backward, and when they paid reverence to the presiding demon they bent themselves backwards, lifting a foot in the air forwards' (H. C. Lea, *History of the Inquisition*, London, iii, 1888, p. 501). A more contemporary account described such a dance in this fashion:

> The dance is strange, and wonderful, as well as diabolical, for turning themselves back to back, they take one another by the arms and raise each other from the ground, then shake their heads to and fro like Anticks, and turn themselves as if they were mad. (*Pleasant Treatise of Witches*, London, 1673, p. 6.)

It appears that this dance survived even to modern times among children in the Walloon districts of Belgium. One common feature is that, at a particular point in the proceedings, the dancers strike their backs or backsides together in time to the music, a kind of early 'boomps-a-daisy'.

One characteristic of the witches' dancing was its liveliness; no one was allowed to fall behind. A 'vice-Devil' was often stationed at the rear of a follow-my-leader column to see that the laggards kept up with the rest, no matter how furious the pace, or wild and unrestrained the jumping and skipping. It is recorded that in one coven in Scotland, a certain Mr Gideon Penman, who had been a minister in Crighton, was usually 'in the rear in all their dances, and beat up all those who were slow', a custom which Dr Murray suggests may have been the origin of the expression: 'the Devil take the hindmost'.

The jumping and unbridled cavorting was probably more than merely an expression of *joie de vivre*. Among the Samburu of Northern Kenya, such leaping in tribal dances is an aid to achieving a hypnoid state. In their case, only the men are allowed to enter a full trance, possibly because the chiefs would not otherwise be able to control the situation:

> Wives sometimes dance with unmarried Moran, and one could see how many emotional transferences could be built up if trance was freely allowed in mixed dancing. . . . The male dancing was far more energetic and so led on to semi-trance, and full trance in some cases. . . . While the Samburu were over-breathing and harshly expelling their breath, they were also rhythmically dropping back hard on to their heels. The whole movement required much muscular effort and obviously would soon start bodily and nervous exhaustion.

The observer here, Dr William Sargant, showed a film of this nomadic dancing to a research bio-chemist, who felt that

> if it had been possible to take arterial blood samples, a high degree of blood alkalosis would have been found, leading to brain alkalosis. We know that brain alkalosis tends to produce suggestible behaviour and trance. Undoubtedly the heavy stamping and rhythmic dancing would create more lactic acid in the blood stream, because of the excessive muscular effort involved, which might counteract some of the alkalosis produced by overbreathing. However, the total effect on the biochemistry would still be an increasing tendency to brain alkalosis, which is what is required if a state of trance is to be fairly rapidly induced (*The Mind Possessed*, pp. 116f.)

The sexual motivation of the Samburu women's dancing was plain enough:

> The women particularly wanted my wife to join in the mixed dancing, so to please them she did. After some initial

difficulty in picking up the rhythm, she found that the only way to imitate the dancing was to imitate the movements of sexual intercourse. When she did this, she found that she was moving in the same way as the native women. It is important to remember that sexual intercourse itself produces overbreathing, and leads on to states of excitement, increased suggestibility, feelings of possession of the loved one, and final collapse.

Similar trance-states were observed by Dr Sargant among Christian congregations in Africa, again induced by ecstatic dancing:

The same possession by the Holy Ghost took place, while the male preacher led the congregation in hand-clapping and singing, and members of the congregation were dancing, jerking, shaking and obtaining the 'gift of tongues' so prized as a sign of God's presence by the early Christians and since in many parts of the world.

The custom of the witches' dancing in animal costume had its Palaeolithic counterpart in cave drawings showing dancers similarly dressed. Engravings made on a deer's antler found at Teyjat in the French Dordogne show three small masked dancers disguised as chamois bucks. 'They are jumping in an upright position and their mighty leaps cause the skins to puff out and swirl. The legs of the youthful dancers protrude from under the chamois skins' (Johannes Maringer, *The Gods of Prehistoric Man,* London, 1960, p. 102f.).

Dr Sargant so describes the 'animal dance':

Rhythmic dancing and leaping are among the principal methods of inducing states of ecstasy in which a man feels taken over by a force or being greater than himself. The dancer dressed as an animal, imitating the animal's characteristic movements and sounds, bringing all his mental and emotional resources to bear with intense concentration on pretending to be the animal, can come to feel that he *is* it. He may also feel that he is a supernatural being, a god or spirit, since he is after all in a 'supernormal' state of mind, markedly different from his ordinary, everyday condition. (*op. cit.*, p. '58.)

We may compare the dancing and cavorting of the

Maenads whose worship of the fertility deity Dionysus had much in common with the cult of the witches:

> Clad in fawnskins and taking in their hands the thyrsos, which was a long rod tipped with a bunch of ivy or vineleaves, the god's own potent emblem, and with ivy-wreaths upon their heads, they follow their leader (a priest of the god) to the wildest parts of the mountains, lost in the bliss of the dance. Many carry snakes, wreathed about them, twined in their hair or grasped in the hand as may be seen in the vase-paintings. Their dance is accompanied by the heavy beat of the tympanum ... and the strains of the reed-flute, as well as their own excited shouts and cries. Nothing is lacking which can serve to increase the sense of exaltation and of shedding the self of everyday existence; to the darkness, the music, and the rhythmic dance are added the smoky light of torches and no doubt the god's especial gift of wine. Erotic enjoyment probably also contributed to producing the final state of *ekstasis* (standing outside oneself) and *enthousiasmos* (possession by the god). (W. K. C. Guthrie, *The Greeks and their Gods*, London, 1950, p. 148f.)

The sacred festivals of the Dionysia, if latterly associated with vine-culture, were probably fired by far more potent drugs than alcohol and based upon a very ancient Asiatic fertility religion. The picture drawn for us by Euripides, in his tragedy *Bacchae,* of the god's female devotees, the Maenads, tearing through the pine-forests in uncontrolled sexual abandon may be largely derived from folklore and literary convention, but it had some elements of truth; the scandal these matronly excesses aroused in more restrained circles of Greek and Roman society had real cause. Nevertheless, the cult enjoyed a very long and far-reaching popularity before the theologians and tragedians tamed its young, high-spirited god into a Muse, and the Maenads into a dramatic chorus about as sexually abandoned as Sunday School scholars tripping around the village Maypole.

The Dionysiac revels were held in secret, for the power they evoked was too terrible for the uninitiated to experience, as the prying Pentheus discovered to his cost. As with all true mystery cults, therefore, we lack first-hand evidence for the details of the rites and the drugs that induced their divine intoxication, or 'possession'.

Like the medieval witches of Europe, the Maenads were accused of devouring children. Legend speaks of the women of Argos who refused to acknowledge the divinity of Dionysus; driven out of their minds by the divine madness, they tore to pieces and devoured their own children. The evidence adduced in the trial of one Louis Gaudfrey at Aix in 1610 includes a similarly fictitious account of witches eating children's flesh:

> They provide a banquet, setting three tables according to the three diuersities of the people above named. They that haue the charge of the bread, doe bring in bread made of corne. The drink which they haue is Malmsley. The meat they ordinarily eate is the flesh of young children, which they cooke and make ready in the Synagogue, sometimes bringing them thither aliue by stealing them from those houses where they haue the opportunity to come . . . (Sebastian Michaelis, *Admirable Historie of the Possession and Conversion of a Penitent Woman*, London, 1613, p. 335f.)

The truth behind the Bacchic and witches' 'child-eating' is probably that their cultic feast included a herb which was popularly likened to, or named after, an infant child or animal and that it contained a drug, hallucinatory, stimulatory, and erotically inflammatory, which accounted for the ecstatic state of the participants. The Dionysiac cult has been linked with the worship of the Vedic god Soma through similarities in legend and character, and the Soma, as we have seen, was a divinely-engendered food which brought its partaker into close communion with the god. In view of its recent identification with the Sacred Mushroom, the *Amanita muscaria*, it is interesting to note that the fungus was known in antiquity as 'the little one' (see above, p. 94), and that through its spotted marking it was connected with the panther (cf. its close relation, the *Amanita pantherina*), whose skin the Maenads wore across their shoulders in the fashion of their god (*Sacred Mushroom* . . . p. 125f.).

The witches' Devil frequently appeared to his followers in the guise of a goat, usually black, and in France apparently this animal was sacrificed as a manifestation of the god. Its flesh was burnt and the ashes carefully collected for the 'execution of their pernicious and abominable designs' (Boguet, p. 141), including, as Dr Murray suggests, sprinkling on fields or animals as a fertility charm (*Witchcraft*, p. 160). The descriptions of this goat-devil are remarkably reminiscent of another of the Dionysiac entourage, Pan, who had the legs, horns, and beard of a goat. This god lived on the slopes of Mount Maenalus or Mount Lycaeus in Arcadia, in grottoes where shepherds came to worship him. He made their goats and ewes prolific, and he is usually portrayed as ithyphallic. He delighted in roaming the forests, frisking with the nymphs whom he sometimes terrified with his appearance, giving his name to our word for sudden fear, or 'panic'. He is particularly associated, like the witches' god, with the pipes, or Syrinx. Although his cult was long localised in Arcadia, every region of Greece came to have its own Pan, as the districts of European witchcraft were controlled by their own Devil. In Mysia, the local Pan was Priapus, the phallic god who presided over the fertility of the fields and flocks, and he, as we have seen, again like the witches' Devil, claimed rights over the virginity of his young female devotees.

There is, however, no need to look so far from northwest Europe for a religion that worshipped a fertility deity and whose rites had something in common with medieval witchcraft. The Scandinavian countries in pagan times worshipped the powers of peace and plenty, as well as the gods of war and thunder like Odin and Thor. These more benevolent deities were called the Vanir, and among them were the twin gods Freyr and Freyja, the children of Njord, according to Snorri

Sturluson, the thirteenth-century Icelander scholar to whom we owe most of our understanding of northern mythology. Snorri does not tell us much about them, but it is clear that he regarded them as powerful beings and that Freyja at least was still being worshipped in his day, when Christianity had long been firmly established in north-west Europe. Of the masculine Freyr, he says that he was much loved by the Swedes because 'in his time the people of the land became richer on account of peace and good seasons than ever before'. (See H. R. Ellis Davidson, *Gods and Myths of Northern Europe*, Harmondsworth, 1964, pp. 92ff.).

Freyr's sister-consort Freyja was invoked, along with Frigg (the Germanic Frija, who gave her name to our day 'Friday', dedicated in the Roman calendar to Venus), by women in labour, and Snorri says that she was the most renowned of goddesses, and probably the last of the old pantheon to survive. As a fertility deity with deeply-rooted associations in the soil and home, this persistent popularity is what one might expect among conservative countryfolk. Her father Njord controlled the winds and sea, while Freyr, his son, gave the sunshine and rain to fertilise the earth.

Freyja was the patroness of human love, and, indeed, in myth is characterised as being something of a nymphomaniac; but, like other fertility goddesses, she is also concerned with death. It is said that she received half-share of all who fell in battle, the other half going to Odin the Wise, god of war, who was credited, like his wife Frigg, with great powers of magic.

Another interesting link with the fertility goddesses of eastern cults is that Frigg and Freyja are envisaged as weeping goddesses. Snorri records that Freyja grieved for her lost husband Od, which would seem to bring her into line with those seasonal deities like Ishtar in Mesopotamia, whose consorts died each year with the failing vegetation, and had to be sought in the underworld to ensure their reappearance the following spring.

Freyja's most cherished ornament is the necklace, *Brisingamen,* a necessary part of the symbolic regalia of fertility figurines from the Mediterranean area, at least as far back as 3000 BC. Another of Freyja's possessions is a feather, mentioned several times in her myths, implying that she could assume the form of a bird and fly vast distances. We are reminded once more of the persistent idea of 'flying' witches and their supposed ability to cover vast distances by magical means.

Snorri tells us, indeed, that Freyja was associated with a special kind of witchcraft know as *seithr,* which she taught to Odin's divinely-begotten brood, the Aesir. Mortal exponents of *seithr*-magic were bands of female soothsayers who travelled about the land visiting farmsteads, and offering their mantic services to all who desired them. They were apparently in great demand on festive occasions, and would appear to be referred to in some Norwegian royal chronicles called *Flateyjarbok:*

> At that time wise women used to go about the land. They were called 'spae-wives' and they foretold people's futures. For this reason folk used to invite them to their houses and give them hospitality, and bestow gifts on them at parting. (I, 346.)

Later it appears that the groups of soothsaying women were reduced to single visitors, and an account of such a séance has come down to us in the Saga of Eric the Red (*Eriks Saga Rautha*), the Icelander who discovered Greenland and settled there in the tenth century. In general, it seems that the seeress, or *volva,* as she is called, sat upon a specially-constructed platform or lofty seat, and was sometimes supported in her ritual by a large company who acted as a choir, accompanying her chanting of the spells. Eric the Red states that on the occasion he describes, the *volva* called for a volunteer to sing an invocatory song, inviting the presence of the spirits at the séance. After some search, a young Christian woman was found who had been taught the chant at her mother's knee, and who was persuaded to perform. Afterwards, the *volva* congratulated the songster, declaring that the spirits had come clamouring to hear her voice, and freely divulged their secrets to their mistress. She had thus been able to answer the questions put to her by her audience, and could foretell the young woman's own fortunes in marriage: 'little that she said went unfulfilled'.

The main burden of the *volva*'s soothsaying concerned the well-being or otherwise of the harvests, of special interest to an agricultural society, and such oracular utterances lent their form to many of the ancient poems that have come down to us. They include the seeress's own descriptions of her journeying into the 'other world', through realms of cold and darkness, and through barriers of fire. In this respect, and in her custom of working herself into a state of trance, there is much in the *volva*'s cult that parallels the shamanism of northern Europe and Asia of more recent times (see Chapter Five). There, too, it will be remembered, the seer divines through attendant spirits that accompany his own soul on long journeys while he is in an ecstatic trance. Like the shaman, the *volva* dresses herself in the skins of wild animals, including boots of calfskin, and gloves made of cats' fur.

Cats seem to have played a significant role in the cult of the *volva*'s divine patroness, Freyja. Snorri tells us that the goddess travelled in a carriage drawn by these animals, and we are reminded that the cat figures prominently on the list of the witch's familiars.

Freyja's mode of transport is in line with a recurring theme in Scandinavian fertility mythology, whereby the deity travels around the land in a waggon, harbinger of warmth and plenty. Even as far back as the first century, Tacitus speaks of a goddess in Denmark called Nerthus, representing *Terra Mater*, 'Mother-earth', who visited her people in a sacred waggon. None but the goddess's own priest might touch it, and it was forbidden for anyone to peer inside. When the priest sensed that his mistress had taken her place in the vehicle, he would set out, leading it around the countryside and finding a ready welcome among the people. Wherever he went, 'they do not undertake hostilities nor take up arms; every weapon is put away; peace and quiet then only are known and welcomed'. When the goddess returned to her sanctuary, set in an island grove, the waggon, the cloth that covered it, and some symbol which it contained, were all washed by slaves in a sacred lake. Then, their task done, the menials were themselves drowned. It has been suggested that the island concerned was Zeeland, on which Copenhagen stands, and where Leire, the seat of the Danish kings in early times, was situated.

It seems, then, that the seeresses who travelled alone or in company, and went around farms in Norway and Iceland may have been the last representatives of the fertility goddess in the north, that deity who, according to Snorri, survived last of all the pagan gods.

> We have evidence here for rites in which women were able to participate fully, both as celebrants and as audience, rites bound up with the fertility of the land and also with the rearing of a family and the giving of young girls in marriage. Frigg and Freyja appear to be concerned in some way with such rites; both at times appear as the beneficent goddess helping women and girls at the times of marriage and child-birth as well as shaping the destiny of children. (Davidson, *op. cit.*, p. 121.)

But, as elsewhere with the cult of the Earth-mother, there was a more sinister side to the religion. Being concerned with the dead, it was believed that *seithr* witchcraft could do harm as well as good; it could not only fill the waters of a sound with fish, as is recorded on one occasion in an eleventh-century chronicle (the Icelandic *Landnamabok*, by Ari the Wise), but it could bring about the death of some designated victim.

This malignant aspect of *seithr* is often found in association with a horse-cult, which we know to have been connected with the Vanir. The witch, like the medieval coven's Devil, could assume the form of a horse and crush her quarry to death, a fate said to have been met by one of Sweden's early kings. Similarly, a twelfth-century English chronicle records that the wife of King Edgar was accused of being a witch and changing herself into a horse. However, in this case her purpose was not to inflict injury upon her enemies, but to satisfy her own unnatural lusts, for she was seen by a bishop 'running and leaping hither and thither with horses, and displaying herself shamelessly to them' (*Historia Eliensis*, 11, 56: C. E. Wright, *The Cultivation of Saga in Anglo-Saxon England*, 1936, pp. 158ff.; quoted by Davidson, p. 122).

Again, accusations of bestiality are common in records of medieval witch trials, and recall the slander levelled against Freyja herself that she was wont to stay out at night like a she-goat among the bucks, and that she took on the likeness of a bitch to satisfy her sexual craving. We noted earlier how folklore credits animals with a less inhibited, and thus more rewarding sex-life than can obtain among humans (see above, p. 115).

The most hostile treatment meted out to the Vanir goddess stems, not surprisingly, from Christian sources, such as the writings of the Danish antiquarian Saxo Grammaticus in the twelfth century. He refers to the more sinister side of her cult in terms of such horror and loathing as to distinguish it from any other heathen religion. Like the Inquisitors' records, Saxo's denunciations leave us with the suspicion that much of his ferocity stems from fear of a rival cult, more deeply-rooted in the hearts of countryfolk than could be expected of his own, comparatively new faith imported from the East.

Conclusion:

A Personal Statement

Recently in Britain the newspapers were full of an incident involving the death of a young woman at the hands of her husband. The man had become convinced that he was possessed by evil spirits and had placed himself in the hands of some professional exorcists. After a long and gruelling session by two clerics and their assistants, the man went home and savagely attacked his wife. The police found him wandering through the streets later, naked and bloodstained, proclaiming that he had freed his dear wife, whom he much loved, from the power of Satan. (*The Times* newspaper, 26 March 1975.)

The man was said to have begun attending meetings of a local Christian Fellowship group, which included in its ranks a 'satanist'. According to the prosecuting counsel at the accused's trial, he had 'somehow become involved in witchcraft, which appeared to have a profound effect'. The local Church of England vicar, a Methodist parson, and their wives, 'expelled some forty demons', but, in the words of the vicar's wife, 'the demons of insanity, murder, and violence, had still not been expelled' when the session broke up. The defending counsel described the Christian group as a party of

> tormented souls who simply fed neurosis to a neurotic. In a few short days he was reduced to a homicidal maniac. In that condition he was subjected to grotesque and wicked malpractices posing in the guise of religion. . . . He was made to confess to sins of which he was innocent and was subjected to indignities which defy comprehension. . . . Religion is the key.

The clergy were said to be disturbed by other aspects of the case, since it appeared from the evidence that the Fellowship group concerned practised 'pentecostalism, or charismatic prayer'. This involved the invoking of the Holy Spirit to grant the worshippers certain benefits, including the 'gift of tongues' and other phenomena, in a highly-charged and emotional atmosphere. One expert at the trial suggested that 'exorcism and pentecostalism would be a dangerous mixture, not least for someone mentally ill'. (*The Times*, 27 March 1975.)

Writing in the same edition of this newspaper, Dr William Sargant, whose observations on spiritual possession have been quoted elsewhere in this book, stated:

> there has been an increasing unhealthy interest in recent years in esoteric religious phenomena. This often happens – in cultures as far back as Greece and Rome – where orthodox religions are losing their hold on people's beliefs . . . possession is almost certainly an hysterical phenomenon occurring especially in *normal* overwrought people. . . .

The defence counsel's dictum that 'religion is the key' to this unhappy affair was, of course, a truism. It is, however, a key to much else besides. For millions of people all over the world, religion serves the necessary function of exorcising the devils of accumulated stress, the seemingly inevitable accompaniment to their everyday living. It springs not from some calm, intellectual assent to certain philosophic doctrines, but from the urging of primeval forces that are Man's heritage from millions of years of evolutionary development. It is akin to, and can be as powerfully compulsive as, sex; its effects on the human psyche can also be as fulfilling, and as potentially destructive.

The lesson of this recent tragedy is to remind us that what passes for 'religion' in our western culture, often hardly more than the placid acceptance of certain moral values and the performance of minimal ritual duties, has very little to do with that passionate devotion and hatred that characterises religion elsewhere. We may have found other, safer ways of releasing our inhibited mental stresses, but we should do well to recognise the explosive forces they can generate. Religious ecstasy can be a useful mechanism for relieving our emotion and achieving some kind of inner peace, but before activating that trigger we need to assure ourselves of the effectiveness of our safety precautions.

In communities more used to handling the wilder expressions of religious emotion, the kind of excesses that figured in this exorcism tragedy would normally have been avoided, or at least released into safer channels. Ecstatic trance-states are encouraged only within certain group situations, where the presiding shamans and their assistants can exercise control over the participants; they have learnt through centuries of experience not only how to induce 'possession', but how to lead their followers through the orgasm of release to calmer waters beyond. They would have taken care that the evil spirits had left the Yorkshire scene before allowing their adept home to claw his wife to pieces.

Of course, not all religious emotion needs to be so unrestrainted. The low-key sustained exercise that is more characteristic of western religions can be no less therapeutically rewarding. Nevertheless, there are dangers even in this muted surrender to irrational sentiment that the foregoing chapters should have made us appreciate. The religionist is notoriously ready to credit theological speculations with more certainty than he will allow the most common, demonstrable facts. This suspension of normal critical faculties can lead, as the world knows to its cost in human suffering, to macabre and inhuman attitudes on the part of otherwise reasonable people. The witch-hunts we have noted should not have been possible among civilised nations with thousands of years of intellectual and humanitarian achievement behind them. Yet normally kind and responsible citizens stood by and watched old women and children burn in their market-places to placate their god, and even today we need not look far to see the most appalling violence perpetrated almost daily in the cause of bigoted sectarianism.

No less dangers await the unwary religionist on his own account, however carefully he may control his outward emotions, and however genuine may be his charitable intentions towards his fellows. The pious believer has to be constantly on his guard against spiritual pride, particularly that inverted kind that thrives on constant self-reproach and self-denigration. Confession and penance may be valuable disciplines for the soul, but absolution bought with martyrdom is too often achieved at the cost of neglected family responsibilities and strained human relationships.

If, then, there is a need in *Homo sapiens* for some periodic, therapeutic release of inner tensions, we may ask if there is not some more rational means of achieving this end than religious ecstasy and group hypnosis. Many people in this Age of Reason have sought a faith that does not conflict with their intellect, forcing them at some stage to choose between rationality and blind belief. They have tried to discover some means of aligning Man's new-found scientific outlook with old deistic convictions about the moral government of the universe. Where theologians have settled on some working compromise, it has usually been achieved by agreeing to divide the spheres of responsibility, rather than by the discovery of some clearly-demonstrable design and purpose in creation. For, however sympathetically one tries to view the processes of biological evolution, it can hardly be claimed an overwhelmingly successful or economic enterprise. It is inordinately wasteful in time, matter, and energy. One is forced sadly to acknowledge that if its purpose was to produce a self-sustaining, self-conscious, intelligent organism in the most efficient way possible, it was both ill-conceived and hopelessly executed from the start, and so far has proved an expensive failure. The whole trial-and-error selective mechanism of our evolutionary system, the process of mass cell-division and chance genetic mutation, is an economist's nightmare. If we are to believe that the Designer of the universe, if he exists, had something more worthwhile in mind than a huge, celestial practical joke, then his purpose was more profound, and devious, than the creation of *Homo sapiens* as an end in itself. The nature of that divine intent has engaged the minds of philosophers ever since Man found time to spare from the necessities of reproducing and feeding himself.

In the meantime, we are all busy devising new ways of preventing our already over-expanded population from succumbing to the one clearly discernible and inexorable law of nature, that the wages of sin – that is, the plunder of natural resources beyond their capability of regeneration – is death. And since any solution to this problem must involve further restrictions upon our freedom to follow our own inclinations, the stresses that already threaten our individual and social stability must increase still further. Primitive tribes find relief for their emotional tensions in ecstatic states achieved under ritually-controlled conditions; they suspend their normal activities for long enough to indulge together in an orgy of discharged emotion and sacrificial drama, and then go back home fulfilled and at peace with themselves, their gods, one another. Unfortunately, civilised man is steadily demythologising his gods out of existence and converting his temples into boot-and-shoe warehouses. He then has to seek in vain for his inner peace on the psychiatrist's couch, in periodic alcoholic 'benders', or, more dangerously, by recourse to drugs.

It may be, then, that, despite our rightly-prized rationality, religion still offers Man his best chance of survival, or, at least, of buying himself a little more time in which to devise some more reasoned way out of his dilemma. If so, it must be a faith that offers something more than a formal assent to a set of highly speculative dogma about the nature of God and His divine purpose in creation; it must promise its adherents a living relationship that answers Man's individual needs within a formal structure of communal worship. It has to satisfy the emotions without violating the believer's intellectual integrity, and it must avoid the tragic divisiveness of ethnic or social affiliations by finding a common reference in our biological heritage. We all travelled the same evolutionary road to manhood and so share the same deep sensibilities about such matters as the good earth, sexual and family relationships, and a due regard for the balance of nature. Racial, climatic, and geographical differences have imposed local variations on Man's responses to these fundamental perceptions, but in the depths of his consciousness there is a common awareness of basic needs and responsibilities. Upon such conceptions it should be possible to found some universal and cohesive faith. Historically, the cult of the Earth-mother has probably come nearest to fulfilling this role, and, being sexually orientated, it has been especially concerned with this most disturbing and potentially disruptive element in Man's biological constitution. Perhaps in our present concern for ecological conservation, with its constant cry for preserving this or that species of wild-life, we are moving towards a revival of the old Nature religion, and re-discovering in the terrestrial womb that gives us birth the allegiance we owe to our lost gods.

Index